Welfare

NICHOLAS RESCHER

WELFARE

The Social Issues in Philosophical Perspective

UNIVERSITY OF PITTSBURGH PRESS

Library of Congress Catalog Card Number 70-158184
ISBN 0-8229-3233-4
Copyright © 1972, University of Pittsburgh Press
All rights reserved
Henry M. Snyder & Co., Inc., London
Manufactured in the United States of America

The quotations from *Essays on "The Welfare State"* by Richard M. Titmuss are used by permission of the publisher, George Allen & Unwin Ltd.

The quotations from *The Other America* by Michael Harrington are used by permission of the publisher, the Macmillan Company, © 1962, the Macmillan Company.

FOR MARK
multum in parvo

Contents

Preface

THIS BOOK SEEKS to appraise the concrete social issues relating to human welfare in a philosophical perspective. In this regard one word of apology seems in order. I am, by trade, a philosopher. Now philosophers are notoriously loath to come to grips with the empirical details of transient circumstances. It is their leading aspiration to deal with timeless truths viewed *sub specie aeternitatis.* This ideal strikes me as neither plausible nor even feasible in political and social philosophy. For the pivot point of all discussion in this region is human well-being and happiness, and this poses issues shot through with empirical detail. The point has the impressive support of Immanuel Kant:

> The concept of happiness is so indefinite that, although each person wishes to attain it, he can never definitely and self-consistently state [*in abstracto*] what he really wishes and wills. The reason for this is that all elements which belong to the concept of happiness are empirical, i.e., they must be taken from experience.[1]

In social philosophy the actualities of empirical circumstances must ever predominate. Accordingly, in writing this discourse on welfare the *Statistical Abstracts of the United States* have ever been kept in reach, and I have been constantly mindful of the soil of the empirical data in which any fruitful consideration of this problem area must root.

1. *Foundations of the Metaphysics of Morals* (Akad. ed., p. 418), trans. L. W. Beck (New York, 1956).

I have, moreover, transgressed the boundaries of philosophical etiquette in yet another way. According to the usual philosophers' conception of good form, it is crucial to keep a high wall of separation not only between theoretical analysis and empirical detail but also between theoretico-descriptive issues on the one hand and normative issues on the other. In the present context, however, these orthodox proprieties seem to make little sense. With welfare—and its principal congeners, such as health and poverty—the normative and the descriptive are so closely interwoven that it becomes a matter of prolix pedantry to attempt to keep the two apart. That the (descriptive) conditions making for illness or impoverishment are also (normatively) bad is so striking and obvious that to keep these aspects antiseptically separated is an exercise in futility. In this work, as in any really useful study of social philosophy, fact and theory, as well as description and assessment, are allowed to operate in seemingly natural and hopefully fruitful symbiosis.

Chapter 3 incorporates some material from an address entitled "Social Values and Technological Change" presented at a centennial symposium at Loyola University in Chicago and scheduled to appear in the forthcoming *Proceedings* of this occasion. In those few other cases where the book draws upon my published writings, specific acknowledgment is made in the footnotes.

Several persons have read parts of the book in manuscript and I have profited from their extensive comments and criticisms. I am in this way indebted to several of my Pittsburgh colleagues, especially Kurt Baier and Alexander Michalos. I want also to express my thanks to Kathy Walsh for her patient help in preparing the typescript through several drafts and revisions.

Nicholas Rescher

Pittsburgh
Spring 1971

Introduction

THIS BOOK IS AN EXAMINATION of key issues of social philosophy centering around the topic of human welfare. Above all, it is a philosophical scrutiny of the objectives of welfare-supportive measures and a critical appraisal of their efficacy for the realization of human happiness. Its approach accordingly combines a soft-hearted concern for human welfare with a hardheaded evaluation of the limits and liabilities of welfare-supportive action at the governmental level.

One of the central themes of the book is an exploration of how the very concept of *public* or *social* "welfare" has changed over the years. The nineteenth century began with the conception of "the minimal state" concerned with the "welfare" of the society in the sense of its *physical security* (law and order, public safety, military security). In the first half of the twentieth century, "the welfare state" came to concern itself with "welfare" in a sense that includes also *economic security* and its requisites (health, education, employment, guaranteed income). In the affluent, technologically sophisticated society of the second half of the twentieth century, the conception of "the managed society" of the "social engineers" will come into prominence, designed to concern itself with "welfare" in a greatly expanded sense. An examination is made of the far-reaching (and by no means uniformly desirable) implications of this vast expansion in the conception of the *social welfare,* and the corresponding extension in the conception of public and governmental responsibility for its achievement.

Extrapolating forward from this historical perspective, it is possible to foresee the ending of the heyday of the welfare state and the coming of an era of diminished social emphasis on catastrophe avoidance and lessened preoccupation with the implementation of minimal uniform standards of adequacy. It is reasonable to expect to find in this new context a heightened social concern—in decentralized and pluralistic patterns—for a more positive and enhanced realization of human potential. This, at any rate, is the perspective that guides the present approach.

A prime objective of the book is to argue several heretical theses, specifically including the following: That men are not necessarily or generally the best judges of their own welfare. That even for a single person, the relationship between his personal welfare and his personal happiness may be a very loose one—so loose as to break apart altogether. That there are sound reasons of general principle for thinking that welfare-supportive programs as presently conceived will fail to achieve professed objectives. That democratic processes are far from being unfailing guarantors of the general welfare. That welfare as a social value is in any event no be-all and end-all, but a desideratum of very limited scope. That important political values, such as freedom and justice, can come into conflict with collective welfare and, on occasion, should properly triumph over it. That the welfare state is not the pinnacle of political evolution, but a stage of development that can *and should* be transcended. Some of the principal assumptions and dogmas of traditional democratic theory and classical liberalism are called into question, despite a fundamental agreement in the ultimate goals that thinkers in this tradition have sought to secure.

However, the book does not argue such heresies on the basis of any outlandish social theories of its own, but rather it supports them on the basis of commonsense and almost truistic premises widely shared among the vast majority of ordinary, well-intentioned people within the mainstream of political life in our time. All the same, I hope that it will stimulate discussion and controversy about the important issues with which it deals.

Welfare

ONE

The Nature of Welfare

1. Man's Welfare

THE WORD WELFARE ultimately derives its current meaning from the original root sense of "having a good trip or journey," conveying the central idea of traveling smoothly on the road of life.[1] Correspondingly, the idea of the *general welfare* relates to what is for the public or common good, *pro bono publico* as the Romans put it.[2] One dictionary defines *welfare* as the "state of faring, or doing well; state or condition in regard to well-being: especially conditions of health, happiness, prosperity, or the like."[3] On the negative side, welfare contrasts with the now obsolete conception of *ilfare*, of having one's affairs fare ill.[4] On closer scrutiny of the concept, it emerges that welfare relates to the *basic requisites of a man's well-being* in general, but most prominently includes those basic concerns with health and economic adequacy within

1. Thus note the German *Wohlfart*.
2. Though the *idea* of the general *welfare* is certainly accessible to others, English has the uncommon advantage of a special term; elsewhere one speaks of "the public weal" (*das allgemeine Wohl*) or "the general good" (*das gemeine Beste, le bien général*). The word *commonweal* initially had a dual sense, denoting the *commonwealth* (the body politic) on the one side and *the common weal* (the general good) on the other. For the interrelationships of these concepts in British political theory of the seventeenth century, see S. T. Bindoff, *Tudor England* (London, 1950), pp. 129–30.
3. *Webster's New International Dictionary*, 2d. ed., s.v. "welfare."
4. As in the 1599 source quoted in the *OED* for the phrase, "Whereupon dependeth either the welfare or ilfare of the whole realm" (*Oxford English Dictionary*, s.v. "welfare").

the range of application to which we have become accustomed by such presently current terms as the "welfare state" or a "welfare worker." This characterization—with its explicit reference to the basic—makes transparently clear one critical negative feature of welfare in its relationship to human well-being in general, namely, that welfare is a matter of "well-being" not in its global totality but in its "basic requisities," its indispensable foundations.[5]

Like health, perhaps its pivotal component, welfare relates to the condition of a person in a certain period of time. When he is well and healthy, well-off and doing well—when in short he is *faring well* in the relevant respects—we say that he is favorably circumstanced in point of welfare. But, of course, welfare is something vastly more many-faceted than health. Welfare has close connections with the conception of a *standard of living*, provided that what is at issue in such a standard is conceived broadly; not simply in terms of consumption levels alone, but in terms of access to essential services and the creation of an adequate—or at least viable—human and natural environment. Since welfare relates to the availability of the basic requisites for human well-being, it points toward the idea of a certain minimum level in the standard of living: any failure to achieve this level is thereby to be viewed as creating a corresponding deficiency in point of welfare. The problem of specifying the setting of such a level, particularly in the pivotally important economic sector of welfare, is obviously a major issue in the theory of welfare.

Since human well-being is a thing of many dimensions, the "welfare of a person" has a plurality of components. Preeminent among these are his *physical* welfare (health), his *material* welfare (prosperity), and even his *spiritual* or psychological welfare (state of mind or "mental health"). Physical health, material circumstances, and mental and emotional well-being are the key elements of welfare. The dictionary definition cited above is rather

---

5. This basicity is stressed by virtually all writers on the subject. For example, "The welfare state is the institutional outcome of the assumption by a society of legal and therefore formal and explicit responsibility for the *basic well-being* of all of its members" (Harry K. Girvetz in *International Encyclopedia of the Social Sciences*, s.v. "Welfare State" [my italics]).

misleading with respect to happiness. Happiness, clearly, is not a *component* of welfare, but its *goal*. One feels that the man whose welfare is in good order, who is healthy, prosperous, and secure is—or ought to be—happy, being possessed of what general consensus regards as the principal requisites of well-being and the prime ingredients of a happy life.

With respect to its components, welfare has the character of a *profile* rather than of an *average*. Just as the health of a person is not an average of the state of health of the various organs and subsystems composing his physical frame, so a person's overall welfare is not an average of his welfare condition in point of the various applicable dimensions: physical, material, psychological, and so on. And just as the lowest point of the health profile, so to speak, represents the focal point around which a man's overall health pivots, so the weakest spot in a person's welfare profile is the critical factor in the on-balance condition of his welfare at large. Like health, welfare is a chain whose strength is determined by its weakest link. Deficiencies in one place are generally not to be compensated for by superiority in another: there are few, if any, tradeoffs operative here—just as cardiovascular superiority does not make up for a deficient liver so added strengths in one sector of welfare cannot cancel out weaknesses in another.[6]

Significant complexity affects the concept of welfare through its psychological dimension; this at once leads to a multitude of ramifications. If physical and material welfare alone were in question, the issue would be a substantially simpler one, since there desiderata can be assured a man in isolation, without overt reference to his significant social relationships. But the whole sector of a man's relation to his fellows, his personal and close-range interactions (in family contacts, professional interactions, friendships, and other human relationships), is a key aspect of his well-

6. Though in essentials, I think, correct, the "profile" versus "average" distinction is not applicable to welfare in a totally unqualified way, since there will no doubt be at least some tradeoffs in this area. A worker, for example, may put up with very dull work (so paying in coin of psychological welfare) to achieve higher pay (for greater returns in terms of material welfare). The point is not that there are never tradeoffs at all, but that there is not enough to make it plausible to approach the matter in terms or an average (of some sort) rather than a profile.

being: the needs about which a man's welfare revolves certainly include those for social interaction with others.[7] Welfare is a matter of the basic requisites of well-being, and man is so constituted that he cannot achieve this condition without reference to the condition of those about him. Since man is a social animal, his own welfare is bound up with that of others with whom he deals at firsthand and who constitute the cast of characters of his life's drama. This involvement with the welfare of others is not an *addition* to a person's welfare; it is, rather, an integral component thereof. A man's welfare certainly, to some extent, comprises—and as it were, internalizes—that of his more intimate associates. A threat to the welfare of his family and friends is transmitted through the linkages binding them together to become a threat to his own welfare as well. This aspect of internalization inescapably endows the welfare of individuals with a social dimension. A man's first-order, self-oriented interests are only part of the range of factors that determine his welfare, which also has its second-order, other-directed component through his involvement with family, friends, etc. Thus first-order welfare interests of others may definitely figure among the second-order welfare interests of a person.

Moreover, welfare has not only a personal but also a wider social aspect. Every person, of course, has his complex of individualized needs whose accommodation is required for the realization of his happiness. But there are also the social needs of people relating to the establishment of a shared social order conducive to their attainment of those requisites for happiness that virtually all people have in common with one another. Two considerations are primarily at issue here. Social welfare relates in general to the social order as an instrumentality for promoting the common, shared individual-welfare needs of the members of the society. More particularly, however, social welfare relates to the social order as promoting those aspects of personal welfare that arise with multiperson involvements, such as shared enterprises and

---

7. Even the "loner," who is sufficient unto himself, has his welfare augmented through the existence of options for a more social mode of life—though he may well choose not to exercise them.

situations of social interaction, in matters ranging from the creation of public resources enjoyed in common (such as a network of roads) to the pleasures of social contact among friends and associates. All the same, the social welfare cannot simply be equated with the social aspect of the individual's welfare, partly because we would need the fiction of the "average man" (a somehow archetypical individual), but mainly because the social welfare comprises those systematic interrelationships that can come into being only through the *interaction* of individuals.

Are a man's education and its correlates, such as intelligence, knowledge, and cultivation, to be regarded as components of his welfare? The answer must be a distinctly qualified affirmative. Clearly we must regard as matters of welfare those minima of schooling and training required to make it possible for a man to function effectively among his fellows under the conditions of their common social environment. And, of course, as this context grows more complex and sophisticated, the intellectual resources needed for adequate participation therein grow correspondingly larger, and the minima at issue look increasingly less insignificant. Welfare is a matter of the resources that a man needs for an at least minimal success in "the pursuit of happiness." Certainly his intellectual and social resources will play a significant role here in addition to physical resources (health) and his material resources (wealth). The intellectual aspect of education is not the pivotal issue here—that is, the acquisition of information and technique—to the exclusion of its moral aspect, especially in the formation of habits of action and attitudes of mind. Moreover, an obvious and close relationship does exist between the education and the economic sectors of welfare, because successful participation in a complex economy crucially depends upon educational preparation.[8]

The key fact is that welfare is composite, complex, and many-sided, and one must consequently resist the simplistic temptation to treat some part of it (the economic or the medical or whatever)

8. The relationships between educational and economic achievement are explored with precision and ingenuity in G. S. Becker, *Human Capital*, National Bureau of Economic Research, General Series, no. 8 (New York, 1964).

as the whole. Yet it is important to recognize that despite its diversified and multifaceted character, the issue of a man's welfare has a certain *minimality* about it. Welfare—in all its dimensions—deals only with the basic essentials. Insofar as the distinction between the basics and the superfluities—the necessities and the luxuries, the minimal *needs* and the nonminimal *desiderata* with respect to the constitution of a man's well-being—is operative in human affairs, welfare relates to the former items alone, without entering into the wider region indicated by the latter ones. Thus while the components of welfare represent great, indeed essentially indispensable, assets to "the good life," they yet furnish no more than the beginnings of such a life. To possess the elemental requisites for something is not necessarily to have the thing itself. The conception of the good life represents a comprehensive whole whose range extends far beyond the core issue of welfare. The man whose cultural horizons are narrow, whose physical environment is unattractive, or whose government is despotic may not actually suffer privation in any of the dimensions of his *welfare*—indeed, he personally may conceivably even be every bit as "happy" as otherwise. Nevertheless, we could not view his condition in point of well-being with unqualified favor and esteem his as "the good life." Welfare is only the *foundation* of such a life, not the structure itself. Physical health, adequacy of resources, and mental and emotional well-being are enormous—perhaps even indispensable—aids toward a meaningful and satisfying life, but they are not in themselves sufficient for this purpose. This is the reason why the components of the good life must extend far beyond the province of welfare. It is essential to keep these considerations in mind from the very first, lest one exaggerate the role of welfare and take it to cover more than the distinctly minimal range with which it is in fact concerned.

2. *Yardsticks for Welfare*

The problem of determining the extent to which the welfare of a person or group is achieved raises at once the question of the *criteria* to be used in evaluating people's welfare standing. In view

of the multidimensionality of welfare, it is inevitable that a wide variety of criteria will be operative. For each of the various dimensions of welfare (health, prosperity, etc.), there will be a long list of particular reference factors to serve as parameters of measurement, for example, in health, such items as life expectancy and external normality. The evaluation of any factor is but one element of the synoptic, overall assessment of a person's welfare status in point of the dimension at issue, be it health, prosperity, etc. Some of these reference factors may be measurable numerically (e.g., a person's life expectancy); others may only admit of a rougher comparative evaluation (e.g., a person's general feeling tone in terms of absence of pain or physical distress). Of course, in assessing a person's overall welfare standing, all these factors must be taken into account within the total welfare profile.

Before making an at least minimally brief survey of these yardsticks, some preliminary remarks are in order. One important point is that satisfaction of these criteria for the realization of personal welfare is not part of the *meaning* of "welfare" (any more than the meaning of "acid" or of "pressure front" has as its part the behavior of the litmus paper or of the barometer we use for its determination). These factors do not define the meaning of "welfare," but rather serve as standards, as mere *tests* for assessing the degree of a person's welfare.

It would be unrealistic, moreover, to conceive of welfare as an essentially instantaneous condition devoid of temporal ramifications. In assessing a man's welfare we would not just take into account his present state, but his foreseeable future prospects as well. Consider a man whose great wealth (say) was threatened by lawsuits or one whose poor circumstances were due for sharp revision in the light of glowing prospects. It would clearly be inappropriate to assess material welfare solely on the basis of the *existing* conditions without reference to future developments. Predictable future eventuations must be reflected in the assessment of a man's *present* welfare condition: one need not wait to take them into account until their impact actually hits him.[9]

9. "As far as our nature as sensible [contrast *rational*] beings is concerned, our happiness is the only thing of importance, provided this is judged, as reason es-

According to Jeremy Bentham, "the value [i.e., measure] of a pleasure or pain considered *by itself* will be greater or less according to the four following circumstances: (1) its *intensity,* (2) its *duration,* (3) its *certainty or uncertainty,* (4) its *propinquity or remoteness* [i.e., in time]."[10] The factors that affect a man's welfare interests would have to be assessed in a very similar way. Any moot developments relevant to a man's welfare can be appraised along such lines, and a comprehensive evaluation requires that all of them—the future-oriented ones specifically included—should be taken into appropriate account.

To develop the criteria of welfare assessment, it is advantageous to begin with the general idea of *elemental requisites for happiness.* As stressed above, welfare figures on the side of essential requirements rather than inessential wants.[11] A man's welfare is a matter of his resources for the satisfaction of his needs: biological, material, social, and—given the nature of his life environment—even intellectual. And, moreover, the promotion of welfare is not a matter of *removing* or suppressing these needs by such substitutes as asceticism or drugs or drink but of "satisfying" them. The aim is not to achieve a certain state—euphoria or contentment—regardless of the means: the "normalcy" of the means to its realization[12] is itself an essential aspect of welfare.

All of the elements of welfare are matters of more or less and so of degree or of comparative extent—a fact that yields good reason for speaking of "yardsticks" for the "measurement" of welfare. The various aspects of a person's health, prosperity, and environmental resources can be measured in statistical terms. The

---

pecially requires, not according to transitory sensation, but according to the influence which this contingency has on our whole existence and our satisfaction with it" (I. Kant, *Critique of Practical Reason* [Akad. ed., p. 61], trans. L. W. Beck [New York, 1956], p. 63).

10. *Principles of Morals and Legislation* (Oxford, 1892), chap. 4.

11. Social philosophers work this distinction hard, though we need not follow them a great way here. The relevant considerations are well set out in S. I. Benn and R. S. Peters, *Social Principles and the Democratic State* (London, 1959), see esp. chap. 6, sec. III, "To say that a man *wants* food is simply to describe his state of mind; to say that he *needs* food is to say that he will not measure up to an understood standard unless he gets it."

12. An idea, no doubt, of endless complication.

relevant procedures are quite obvious with factors like wealth or life expectancy, and less obvious but no less feasible with factors like the quantity and intensity of a man's interpersonal relationships.

This fact that the aspects of welfare are matters of degree has far-reaching consequences for the specification of welfare standards; these can consequently be set in either absolute or comparative terms. In the former (absolute) case, we moot the issue of *how favorably or unfavorably a man is circumstanced* in point of welfare considerations, namely, how healthy or prosperous he is, and the like. In the latter (relative or comparative) case, we moot the issue of *how much more or less favorably as compared with others* a man is circumstanced in the relevant respects. For example, regarding wealth we might indicate either (1) how much a man has or (2) how much better (or worse) off he is than others. In a very affluent society, a man might possess a great deal and yet be in the lowest wealth quartile. In a very poor society, he might have very little and yet be in the top 10 percent. And this situation is typical: the two sorts of welfare standards work independently of one another, and to give a fully meaningful picture of the situation, measurements should be made according to both relative and absolute criteria.

The questions of "How much has he?" or "How much more or less has he in comparison with others?" or "How much more or less has he in relation to what he wants (or what he thinks he ought to have)?" pose very difficult issues. With this latter question we leave behind the sphere of *needs* and enter that of *expectations* and *aspirations*. At this point we turn away from basics and minimalities and, departing from the issue of welfare as such, go over to that of an enhanced vision of the good life. We have stepped outside the relatively public and objective domain of welfare to enter that of private views and personal attitudes.

The task of welfare appraisal opens up in its public and objective mode the whole area of the use of statistics as a means of comparing and contrasting the condition of different individuals within a wider social setting. The statistical nature of various measures of social welfare such as "life expectancy" or "the standard of living" is too well known to need elaboration. The very concepts commonly employed in thinking about issues of social welfare—mortality rates, crime, indices, length-of-schooling curves, and the like—were not available until relatively recently. It is close to inconceivable that anything approaching the welfare-oriented society of recent decades could have come about before the age of social statistics—especially in the economic and medical areas. (This key theme of "social indicators" will have to be resumed later in considerable detail.)

After these preliminaries, we can settle down to the survey of the main yardstick for welfare. The principal criteria for assessing the degree of realization of a man's welfare can be outlined as follows:

I. Physical health
   A. Life expectancy
   B. Physical condition (vigor, adequacy of functioning)
   C. Physical feeling tone (absence of pain or physical distress)
   D. External normality (absence of disfigurement and overt physical impairment or disability)
II. Mental health
   A. Capacity to act effectively along chosen lines in chosen directions (outside controlled, limited, or institutional contexts)
   B. Mental tone (absence of abnormal fears, animosities, mental distress and connected symptomology, etc).
   C. Satisfaction with himself and his circumstances (self-respect and contentment)
   D. Capacity to function normally in interpersonal transactions
III. Material prosperity
   A. Income
   B. Possession of negotiable assets (money, land, negotiable securities)
   C. Access to the services of others
   D. Security in tenure of material possession

IV. Personal assets
   A. Intellectual resources (cf. II.A)
   B. Social resources (cf. II.D)
V. Environmental resources[13]
   A. Availability of goods for personal use
   B. Availability of personal services
   C. Quality of the environment (artificial and natural, social, public health, etc.)

A long commentary could—and ideally should—be written about each of these items, but we shall limit ourselves to some brief remarks about a few of them. One striking thing is that the items of the first catagory (physical health) in large degree lack intimate interconnections with one another. For example, a person in good physical condition may have some subsurface malady that impairs his life expectancy, or he may suffer from some painful or debilitating condition that leaves his life expectancy unimpaired (e.g., arthritis). Unlike the items at issue in the other categories, where there are strong interdependencies among the subordinated groupings, the factors belonging to the first category are relatively independent.

The environmental assets represent an especially important category. The welfare of a relatively poor city dweller can be augmented in a comparison with his small-town cousin by easier access to better medical, educational, and cultural facilities. On the other hand, the small town may well provide a better physical environment (less noise, traffic, human congestion, better air, more trees, etc) and in some circumstances a more congenial social environment as well. Obviously, various localities will differ greatly in this respect—who could fail to be impressed with the greater surface pleasantness of Amsterdam in contrast with Chicago,

---

13. There are certainly problematic cases here. For example, is "what other people think of him"—his *reputation* or "good name and fame" beyond the level demanded for minimal essential dealings with others—to be counted among a person's environmental assets (or, for that matter, his *power* over others)? The answer is, of course, affirmative, but clearly not all of a person's assets are aspects of his welfare. (Thus urbanity and refined culture are personal assets, but lie outside the welfare sector.) Here only those environmental assets are considered relevant that themselves relate to the other dimensions of welfare.

Vienna in contrast with Boston, Berne or Geneva in contrast with Pittsburgh or Detroit?

Category III (material prosperity) is different from the rest in an important respect. Learning, the cultivation of health in its various forms, and the enhancement of environmental assets all are essentially cooperative enterprises rather than competitive ones. Material prosperity, however, has a significantly competitive dimension. This area of welfare exhibits the striking phenomenon that one person's welfare be promoted at the expense of that of others; in the other areas, a person's promotion of his welfare is, at worst, indifferent to the realization by others of their own welfare interests—and often positively conducive to it.

In considering group welfare, we confront the difficult problem of determining *the role of different individuals in the "sum" of a group's overall welfare status.* Formulated in such abstract terms, the problem seems barren and academic. That it can become very real is readily brought out by an example. Is the welfare condition of a group improved or the reverse by a measure that brings a small benefit to many and a substantial detriment to a few—say, by a public-health measure that for most individuals decreases very slightly the probability of contracting a common cold but has seriously detrimental consequences for a few individuals, say only the one in a million who has some rare biomedical condition? We could readily set the problem up in life-expectancy terms. Suppose the measure increases the life expectancy of "normal" people by .001 days but decreases that of people in the rare condition by one year. Then, in a city of 10,000,000 population, introduction of the measure would lead to roughly 10,000 more expected man-days of life on the part of the "normal" people and would lead to 3,650 fewer expected man-days of life on the part of those in the very rare condition. Would the expectation of an added 6,350 life-days automatically vindicate introduction of the measure on grounds of increased welfare? That this is so is very far from evident. The entire problem of how group welfare relates to the welfare of individuals is a thorny theoretical issue whose Gordian knot the political process more often cuts than unravels.[14]

14. For a discussion of key issues see Nicholas Rescher, *Distributive Justice* (New York, 1966).

We have argued that a person's welfare is a matter of a profile rather than an average. This means that the adequate support of welfare requires action pretty well all along the line—and, above all, at the weakest points of the overall structure. The support of welfare is a matter of maintaining a suitable *balance* among its components to keep them in proper proportion. It is illuminating to view in this light the key thesis of J. K. Galbraith's influential book, *The Affluent Society*.[15] Americans, so Galbraith argues, have been too concerned with expending their national affluence in the private sector of personal goods and services and have made no comparably adequate investment in the support of the public sector of environmental assets. The resulting decline of public facilities and services have created the paradoxical juxtaposition of private wealth and public squalor—of investment in luxury cars and vacations on sunny California beaches by people living in dirty cities unsafe from criminal attack. Viewed from our present angle, Galbraith's diagnosis reveals an imbalance in the welfare profile—an undue stress upon the material as compared with the environmental sector of personal welfare.

3. Who's to Judge?

The issue of who is the best judge of a person's welfare—who is best qualified and most competent to make assessments regarding welfare—is central to a proper understanding of what welfare is all about. The exploration of this problem not only throws light upon some key aspects of welfare itself, but also helps in resolving some of the main difficulties encountered in this area.

A deep-rooted feeling is unquestionably present in most well-meaning people that no one can have a better understanding of the issues relating to person's own affairs—and, above all, those regarding his own welfare and well-being—than the man himself. This creditable sentiment is supported and fortified by exposure to the widely current liberal, democratic principle that people themselves are necessarily the best judges of their interests. But a thoughtful scrutiny of the facts will not bear out this importation of welfare into the sphere of those subjective items—such as his

---

15. Boston, Mass., 1958.

own likings and preferences—regarding which a person is obviously better qualified to judge than any of his fellows.

It is important in this connection to distinguish between *being informed* and *concern*. No doubt the man himself is in general more concerned about his welfare interests than others, but that certainly does not mean that he is usually better informed about them. Here again the medical analogy is telling: doubtless a man has a greater stake in and is consequently (if reasonable) more concerned about his health than his physician, but his physician will, in general, know a great deal more about the matter.

Fundamental to this entire problem is the critical distinction between subjective states on the one hand and objective conditions on the other. Whether a man "feels cold" or "is worried" or "feels well and healthy" are all, at bottom, subjective factors, in clear contrast to whether it "is cold" (relative to the temperature situation that has generally prevailed in his past), whether he "has cause for worry," or whether he "is actually in good health," all of which are objective conditions of affairs that can be determined without any reference to someone's subjective feelings. This distinction is crucial for present purposes. No doubt, people are the best-qualified judges of their own subjective states, and no one else is in a better position to make judgments about items of this sort than the person himself. But whether that person finds himself in a certain objective condition is best judged by someone with a clear head and a great quantity of relevant information at his disposal, who need by no means be the subject himself—indeed, will generally not be. Such locutions as "He doesn't know what's good for him" and "He doesn't know when he's well off" are by no means pointless. Welfare, moreover, has heavily predictive and future-oriented involvements. Now a man is unquestionably the best judge as to whether or not he *is* happy at present, but others may well be—indeed, quite probably will be—better judges as to whether or not he *will be* happy in such and such presumptive future circumstances.

A person's welfare is a matter of objective conditions and circumstances, not of his subjective state. His material prosperity, his mental health, his physical condition—all these are objective facts that can be as well (or better) known to others as to himself: his family doctor, his financial counselor, his legal adviser, etc. For the state of his welfare—unlike any fleeting feelings of contentment or happiness or elation—is not a transient mental state of subjective psychological mood that the subject himself is, in the very nature of things, best fitted to judge. A person's welfare is determined by his state and condition in certain specifiable and overt respects: health, financial status, and the like. Judgments of welfare are matters of (objective) *knowledge* and not matters of (subjective) *feeling*. Thus whether a person's welfare is in better—or worse—shape than it used to be is an issue about which others may well be better informed than he. Welfare is thus not in any immediate way a matter of psychological feelings or moods or states of mind; rather, it is a function of the extent to which certain objective circumstances are realized, namely, those generally regarded as representing requisites for the achievement of happiness in the existing life environment. Welfare hinges upon objectively determinable circumstances, and a sphere of action is consequently opened up for the effective workings of "outside" expertise.

The case has actually been understated by merely maintaining that a person is himself not necessarily best qualified to assess his own welfare and to judge correctly the factors at issue in it. For not only can someone fail to be well informed in this regard, he can be definitely and seriously mistaken. He may possibly—but very erroneously—feel perfectly assured that the consumption of alcoholic beverages is conducive to the effectiveness of his physical functioning or that his gambling is beneficial to his financial security. Indeed, a person himself may utterly lack the capacity for the realistic assessment of his welfare. Yet this case—though perfectly possible—is certainly not to be view as standard. Admittedly, no one else is more intimately concerned in and more extensively involved with the welfare of a rational adult individual than the person himself. And consequently, we ordinarily make a presumption of competence in this regard: in the absence of any indications to the contrary, we commonly adopt the working principle of viewing our fellows as responsible agents where their welfare is concerned.

One central aspect of being a responsible person is an intelligent solicitude for one's own welfare; and, correspondingly, in treating people as responsible, we "operate on the assumption" that they are capable of making competent judgments in matters of welfare. Nevertheless, a clear sign that people are not to be regarded as *automatically* the best-qualified judges of their own welfare is provided by the case of the intellectually underdeveloped, the immature, or the abnormal—children and the mentally deranged. It would be the height of folly to consider all such people as invariably competent to make appropriate judgment in matters concerning their own welfare. But remark, by contrast, that there is no doubt whatever that even children and madmen are the best judges as to whether or not they *feel* discomfort or pleasure and whether they are happy or miserable. What *pleases* a person, and what he *prefers*, *likes*, or *wants*, is something subjective unto himself, but what is *in his interest* is an objective issue, and welfare goes with the latter category, not the former.

The objectivity of welfare can be driven home by reviewing the yardsticks of welfare set out above. Consider, for example, life expectancy or physical vigor in connection with the dimension of health and prosperity, or control over goods and services in connection with the economic dimension. All such criteria are completely interpersonal and objective in character: their application hinges merely upon having the right information—information of a wholly public sort, to which others may well have easier access than the subject himself. Throughout, we confront factors that are not private and inaccessible but lie open to public evaluation, determinable by anyone who troubles to seek out the proper information. The assessment of a person's welfare status can be carried out with reference to its external aspects and in no way requires us to penetrate his inner feelings or thought-life. Welfare is strictly a matter of outer and public circumstances and requires no direct reference to inner and private moods or feelings.[16]

16. There is, of course, *some* sort of relationship of a very loose and "by and

Welfare is, in this respect, decisively different from well-being as a whole, construed in its full generality and specifically comprising happiness. Only a novelist or biographer of considerable psychological acumen can convey to his reader an adequate picture of the condition of psychic well-being and happiness characterizing his protagonists at a given juncture. But the condition of their *welfare* is something vastly easier to discern. Usually the barest outline of a person's life in a biographical dictionary or an obituary notice is sufficient for a reasonably accurate appraisal of his welfare condition at the various stages of life. The status of a person's welfare is not merely public and objective; it is generally even *superficial* in the literal sense of lying near the surface of observation—for suitably trained observers, at any rate.[17]

What has been said here as to the welfare of an individual holds also for that of a group. People can—and often unhesitatingly do—make judgments regarding the welfare of others living in groups to which they themselves by no means belong. An interesting combination of such appraisals by "outsiders" is afforded in the following passage from J. A. Hobson's classic work, *The Social Problem*.[18] In discussing the condition of the poor in England at the turn of the century, Hobson writes:

The life of these people is not worth living, so far as measurements of life are possible; they are living a life definitely worse in almost all respects than that of "savages" in any fairly fertile land, and with hardly more hope of escape or advancement. Take this statement of a recent traveller in Bechuanaland, only one of many similar testimonies: "I have visited nearly every native town of consequence in Bechuanaland, and I say unhesitatingly that these people are at this moment physically

---

large" sort. An improvement in X's welfare suggests that there is some prospect of an improvement of his inner moods and feelings. Care for the welfare of others would be pointless if there were not at least some prospect of favorably affecting what goes on "inside" them. But the immense tenuousness of the relationship cannot be overemphasized.

17. This superficiality of the relevant considerations explains why the issue of social welfare is so easily explored by relatively simple statistical techniques of the "census" variety. For a helpful exploration of this theme, see David Braybrooke, *Three Tests for Democracy: Personal Rights, Human Welfare, Collective Preference* (New York, 1968), esp. pt. II, chap. 2.

18. New York, 1901.

and morally far better off than many thousands of the population of our great cities in Great Britain, living happier and healthier lives by far than seven-tenths of our poor folk at home."[19]

One need not accept the specific appraisals at issue here to recognize them as instances of that familiar and indeed common phenomenon, an outsider's assessment of the condition of a group's welfare. Just as an individual is not necessarily the best judge of his own welfare, so the members of a group need not themselves be infallible authorities in matters regarding their welfare; in this regard, outsiders can be better informed than they. The "foreign" doctor or economist or anthropologist may well realize better than do the "natives" themselves that existing conditions are in certain respects detrimental to their well-being, and that their state of welfare would be favorably affected by certain changes in their modus operandi.

In making judgments of this sort the outside observer must, of course, have at his disposal a great deal of specific factual information about the group at issue. Recognizing that the external observer may very possibly be in a better position to make an assessment of welfare than the subject himself, it must be stressed that this subject, however, must be the pivot about which these considerations revolve. The assessment of people's welfare is not to be made from some abstract, depersonalized point of view. Welfare certainly has its idiosyncratic involvements—the subject's own tastes, inclination, personality makeup, physical constitution, etc., all potentially serve as reference points relevant to an assessment of his welfare. People differ from one another in their biomedical makeup and their individual psychology, and consequently also in their economic needs (e.g., in providing a particular environment necessary to maintain a person's health).

Judgments regarding the welfare of people, while not subjective, will thus have to be emphatically subject oriented: they require objective information about the specific people in view. In this regard welfare judgments are typified by medical judgments regarding one's state of health. Just as the patient himself is the

19.   Henry A. Bryden, Gun and Camera in South Africa (London, 1893), p. 129.

definitive authority as to "how he feels," so the subject is the definitive authority as to whether or not "he feels content and happy." But this subjective element no more settles a question of welfare in general than one of health in particular.[20] Neither with the state of health specifically nor with the state of welfare at large are feelings definitive indicators of objective conditions. In both cases, information of the sort available not necessarily to the person himself but to an expert outsider provides the crucial basis for judgment. However, this information is in large measure not something general and universalizable; it will hinge critically upon the specific data regarding the characteristic makeup of the particular individual at issue. Workable welfare considerations certainly cannot be excogitated a priori—too much information is required regarding the reactions of specific men operating within specific environmental contexts. Accordingly, reliable welfare judgments are in large measure not matters of general theory but of particular observation and involve a great deal of commonsense knowledge based upon experience regarding the norms and the vagaries of human affairs.

Substantial dangers thus inhere in welfare judgments made by outsiders on a subject's behalf. The dictator, the foreign sociologist, and the government official are all prone to make horrible blunders when they tell themselves (and others), "I know what's best for the people here." This attitude can lead readily to cynical abuse or to myopic paternalism.[21] But to say all this is to say no more than that welfare judgments—like all judgments—can be made badly. In considering the theoretical nature of appraisals of welfare, we must insist upon our paradigm of the medical,

20. The point is reminiscent of Oliver Cromwell's dictum, "What's for their good, not what pleases them—that's the question."

21. "The merit of democracy is that in requiring the would-be legislator to court his constituents, it forces him to examine their needs at close quarters. He must consult their experience, rather than assume, on the strength of his own, that he knows either what they want, or what would be good for them. It would be rash to say that every man knows best what is best for himself; but it is wise nevertheless to ask him what he wants and why he wants it, before concluding that he is mistaken. And this is the minimum compatible with the moral criterion of respect for persons as sources of claims" (Benn and Peters, *Social Principles and the Democratic State*, chap. 15, sec. III c).

economic, or legal counselor. Here, too, mistakes can doubtless occur—but in general are vastly less likely to come from a well-trained, well-informed, and sympathetic outsider than from the subject himself.

The implications of this view that others may well be better judges of a man's welfare than he himself need to be faced with greater explicitness. For let us conjoin this thesis with the further contention—plausible enough in itself—that the state is to bear a substantial responsibility in assuring the welfare of its members. Then it might seem to follow that one must be prepared to hand the affairs of people over to the myrmidons of the state, and to put the management of their lives at the hazard of the technocrats and social engineers who operate the bureaucratic mechanism of the state's welfare-supportive machinery. To understand that this consequence by no means follows, we must recall our previous strictures as to the very limited character of welfare in constituting but one small, albeit foundation, factor in human well-being. For clearly, to assign to the state responsibility for a basic part is not to give it responsibility for the whole. Water is essential to human life; man cannot live without water. Yet to charge a municipality with the maintenances of the water supply, and so to charge it with managing a factor fundamental to the lives of its inhabitants, is not to charge it with the management of their lives as such. It is precisely because welfare is a very incomplete (though, to be sure, important) episode in the overall drama of people's well-being that its involvements with the modern state need not in-evitably—one certainly may not say *cannot possibly*—lead to consequences detrimental to the liberty of the individual.[22]

22. This matter of the state's responsibility for welfare is a large and important theme to which we shall return in chapter 7.

TWO

Social Welfare as a Value

THEIR OWN PERSONAL WELFARE and that of those connected with them has, of course, always been prominent in the minds of most men. But the conditions of life in modern, advanced societies give special prominence to the general welfare upon the stage of contemporary social thought. To understand the proper role of welfare in social ideology, it is useful to view it in its most characteristic setting, by recognizing and examining its prominent position in the framework of *human values*.

Values are intangibles. In the final analysis, they are things of the mind that have to do with the vision people have of "the good life" for themselves and their fellows. Each of a person's values—be it "loyalty" or "economic justice" or "self-aggrandizement"—plays a role in his concept of human well-being by providing a standard by which he assesses the extent of his satisfactions in and with life. Abstract in character, these values manifest themselves concretely in the ways in which people talk and act, and especially in the pattern of their expenditure of time and effort, in their actions at work and leisure, and in their choices in the marketplace. It is primarily through these concrete manifestations that values secure their importance and relevance in human affairs. This, however, does not alter the fact of their own abstract and mentalistic nature, nor does it mitigate their methodologically problematic character.

Let us begin with a calculatedly oblique approach to the question, *What is a value?* Rather than considering what a value *is*, let us first deal with the problem of how a value *is manifested.* How is the presence of a value detected? When we impute subscription to a certain value to someone (be it "love of country" or "devotion to duty" or "the worship of Mammon"), what grounds can we possibly have for this claim?

It is clear that value subscription can manifest itself in two significantly distinguishable overt modes: first on the side of *talk* (or thought), in claiming that a person subscribes to a value, we give grounds for expecting a certain characteristic type of verbal action, namely, that he would "appeal to this value," both in the support and justification of his own (or other people's) actions and in urging upon others the adoption of actions, courses of action, and policies for acting. Moreover, in addition to such overt verbal behavior, we would, of course, expect him to take the value into proper account in the "inner discourse" (*in foro interno*) of deliberation and decision-making. In imputing a value to someone, we advance the claim and underwrite the expectation that its espousal will appropriately manifest itself in his position regarding the justification and recommendation of actions. The prime indicators of value subscription are those items which reflect the *rationalization* (defense, recommendation, justification, critique) of the patterns of activity that constitute aspects of a "way of life." *A value represents a thesis capable of providing for the rationalization of action by conveying a positive attitude toward a purportedly beneficial state of affairs.* This formula accurately indicates the fundamentally ideological character of values: values are banners under which one can fight (however mildly), being bound up with man's vision of the good life through his concept of the beneficial.

People's values function both as constraints and as stimuli. A man's adherence to a certain value, say "patriotism," motivates him in doing some things (e.g., resenting an aspersion upon his country) and in refraining from doing others (e.g., any disloyal action). The prevalent values of a society—particularly of a democratic society—significantly condition the ways it conceives of, and goes about discharging, its business. The flat rejection of the prospect of preventive war by the United States and the no-first-strike policy maintained through several successive administrations—Republican and Democrat alike—reflect in significant part the appreciation by America's political leadership of certain fundamental value commitments of the American people. Values are thus an important element, not merely for the sociologists' understanding of national traits and character, but even for the appreciation of political realities. Values are important for politics, that "art of the possible," because they play a significant role in the determination of what *is* possible within the social framework of a given nation.

So much by way of background regarding values in general. Let us now work our way back to that one value which most concerns us here: the social welfare.

Any cohesive society is certain to have a group of values that occupy a commanding position on its value scale. Insofar as they are not simply taken for granted, these most deeply held values are viewed by the bulk of the society's membership as relatively unchangeable and virtually "beyond dispute." Now in most modern, advanced, Westernized societies—and certainly in the national societies of Europe and North America—these dominant values prominently include: (1) the SURVIVAL of the society, (2) the WELFARE of the society, (3) the ADVANCEMENT of the society, and (4) REALITY ADJUSTMENT of the society.[1]

What is at issue with the first of these values is, of course, not only a matter of the *mere* survival of the society, but of its survival as the sort of society it is; this value is thus a matter of a kind of social homeostasis. The third dominant value, advancement or progress, is primarily a matter of the ongoing improvement of the state of affairs obtaining under the two preceding heads. The fundamentality of this value is bound up with the future-orientedness pervasive in Westernized societies and the prominence of innovative and progressivistic thinking. Finally, reality adjustment is a matter of "accepting things as they are," and adjusting to them if need be, rather than seeking false security in some fantasy realm of myth or magic. If it should happen that the pursuit of

1. For an interesting discussion of cognate ideas, see Talcott Parsons, *Theories of Society* (New York, 1961).

the realization of a value somehow becomes much more difficult or costly so that one must (*ex hypothesi*) "settle for less," one can either adjust and "accept the inevitable," or else keep the lamp of aspiration burning bright, possibly even giving this value a greater emphasis. A culture heavily committed to "reality adjustment" would by and large tend to the first mode of resolution, possibly excepting the case where its dominant and basic values themselves are concerned.

The issue of most concern at present is, of course, that of the key role of welfare as a dominant social value. To begin with, it deserves note that welfare is what might be termed a *package value*. It is a cluster that brings together many values (health, prosperity, etc.), exactly as is the case, for example, with justice, which brings together legality, equity, economic justice, social justice, etc. In another way, too, welfare is a complex composite, for if informed that welfare is among someone's values we will certainly want to know just *whose* welfare is at issue: his own, that of some "ingroup," or that of people in general (the general welfare).

From the standpoint of the values involved, an individual's own welfare is patently on a very different footing from that of the general welfare. Quite obviously, people's own personal welfare and that of those intimately connected with them has always been near the forefront of their thoughts, so that welfare with reference to themselves and their immediately proximate social units has standardly been a key value for individuals. But the joint operation of many causes—most of them fruits of modern technology: affluence, education, communications systems (the "media"), the increase of population densities, etc.—have brought far-reaching changes in this regard. Nowadays people can no longer cultivate their welfare interests in relative independence, and this has endowed the general welfare with a new and unprecedented importance as a social value.

To say that social welfare is *a* key value is not, of course, to say that it is the alpha and omega of value. Both singly and in social aggregates, people have values ranging over a wide front outside the sphere of welfare. The welfare sector deals with issues where—as in economics and public health—the interests of all the people of a society are closely interconnected, so that shared interests can be pursued in common. But the welfare interests of a society are certainly sometimes in fact subordinated to others, more often matters of survival, but sometimes even such a highly ideological objective as honoring one's commitments. Though an important value, welfare is but one among many. And there is no reason of principle why this should not be so: with societies, as with individuals, welfare is no be-all and end-all. But it is very significant and promises to become even more so.

This fact of the increased prominence of social welfare as an individual value points toward the general question, How can a change in the operating environment (the economic, technological, demographic, etc., sector) of a society be expected to work to induce a change in its schedule of values? One important key to this question lies in the observation that when values can come into conflict with one another they do so not in the abstract, but in the competing demands their realization and pursuit make upon man's finite resources of goods, time, effort, attention, etc. Thus when a change occurs in the operative framework within which a value is pursued in a given society, we may expect a series of stresses upon our scale of values militating for a rescaling in their ordering or a change of the value standard, etc. But how is one to determine the character of this value response? Here key factors lie in two considerations: *cost* and *benefit*.

a. *The cost of maintaining a value.* As was just said, pursuit of the realization of a value requires the investment of various resources. The extent of the requisite investment will be affected by changes in the environment: "cleanliness" comes cheaper in modern cities than in medieval ones, and the achievement of "privacy" costs more in urban environments than in rural ones. The maintenance of a value will obviously be influenced by its cost. When this becomes *very* low, we may tend to depreciate the value as such. When it becomes high, we may either depreciate the value in question as such (the "fox and the grapes" reaction) or—rather more commonly—simply settle for lower standards for its attainment. (Think here of "peace and quiet" in this era of jet screams, sonic booms, and auto sirens.)

b. *The felt benefit of (or need for) maintaining a value.* When speaking of the "benefit of" or the "need for" maintaining a certain value in a society, we mean that society to be thought of in terms of its fundamental and dominant values and, in particular, in terms of its survival as the sort of society it is. Thus, for example, "pluralism," which plays such a prominent role in contemporary U.S. Catholic thought, answers to a "need" precisely because it is conducive to the real interests of the group in helping it to operate effectively within the constraints of its environment. Again, "scientific and intellectual skills" and the various values bound up with them are, of late, coming to be upgraded on the American value scale precisely because of society's increased need for these skills in the interests of survival, welfare, and advancement under contemporary conditions. Much the same can be said for "innovation," as witness the really very modest degree of worker resistance to technological change in recent years.

This perspective highlights the idea of the *relevance* of values to the specific life-environment that provides the operative setting within which a value is espoused. For with a change in this setting, a certain value may be more or less *deserving* of emphasis, depending on the changes in the nature and extent of the corresponding benefits in the altered circumstances. Or again, the value may be more or less *demanding* of emphasis, depending on changes in the cost of its realization in a given degree. In extreme cases, a value can become *irrelevant* when the life-setting has become such that the historically associated benefits are no longer available (e.g., knight-errantry, chivalry, and—perhaps—*noblesse oblige*), or it can even become malign when action on it comes to produce more harm than good (as with certain forms of "charity").[2]

These general considerations provide the background against

2. For a further development of the approach to values taken in this chapter, see the author's *Introduction to Value Theory* (Englewood Cliffs, N.J., 1969); the present discussion of values has drawn upon that work.

which one can best understand the increased prominence of the general welfare as a social value. A vast network of interdependencies among the fates of people has been created by the conditions of life in modern advanced societies. Many lives, for example, depend upon each driver's exercise of reasonable care and competence on a modern high-speed highway. Under contemporary conditions, all members of a society are highly interdependent in point of their economic well-being, public health, the condition of the social order, the maintenance of tolerable limits in the condition of their physical environment in the face of air and water pollution, etc. It is essential to the maintenance of a viable life-setting in currently prevalent circumstances that the individual members of the society be duly mindful of the general welfare. *The social welfare of the group* is a pivotal value, adhesion to which by individual members of the group is virtually essential if they are to create and preserve for one another bearable conditions in their common environment. Its importance derives from a very hard-core and rock-bottom consideration: survival. Given the operative setting of contemporary advanced societies, the social welfare plays a pivotal role as a value just because it is highly survival-conducive.

The crowding of the avenues of action in modern life increasingly puts the individual into a position not so much of *interacting* with other individuals as individual agents but of *reacting* to them as a mass comprising a complex "system." Many of the things that go wrong are best looked at—at any rate, from the standpoint of their victims—as *system malfunctions.* It seems probable in this context that we will less and less treat such failures as matters of individual accountability. If X cheats, burgles, or inflicts motor-vehicle damage upon Y, the view will increasingly prevail that Y should not have to look to X for recovery from loss but to a depersonalized source—namely, some agency of the society. We will not improbably move increasingly toward the concept of a "veteran's administration" for the victims of the ordinary hazards of life in our society. Individual responsibility and personal accountability have suffered some depreciation in American life over the past two decades, but it seems likely that in the years ahead social accountability will become an increasingly prominent factor. Irresistible pressures are operative to replace independence by interdependence and to give the general welfare an ideological significance far greater than that which it has enjoyed heretofore.

A concern for others, with its essential reference to the general welfare is certain to become an increasingly necessary factor in the days ahead. Internalization of the interests of others is the central factor in taking what can only be characterized as the *social point of view* in matters of welfare. From this point of view it seems only natural that the social welfare should be one of the pivotal values of modern, advanced societies in general. And, in fact, this concern for social welfare is certainly not confined to the orbit of democratic nations. The non-Communist West possesses no monopoly on the rhetoric of social welfare. Influential Communist theoreticians and spokesmen nowadays unhesitatingly voice such sentiments as: "Constant enhancement of the welfare of the community has been the prime objective of the Soviet planning system throughout all the periods of Soviet economic development."[3]

The mutuality of interests in the mass, systematized society created by advanced technology assures public welfare of a critical place as a social value. But not only is social welfare enhanced in importance, it is also rendered easier to attain by modern social and technical instrumentalities. This conjoint prospect of realizing increased benefits at relatively decreased cost is bound to assure the general welfare of a substantially higher place in the spectrum of the social values espoused by individuals.

To sharpen this point we shall proceed by taking into view some characteristic cases which can be described simply and with great precision, drawing upon the theory of games. Actually, the point to be made within the area of present purpose involves games of a very simple sort: two-person games, albeit not zero-

3. N. P. Fedorenko (Director of the Central Economic-Mathematical Institute, Academy of Sciences of the USSR, Moscow), "Planning of Production and Consumption in the U.S.S.R.," *Technological Forecasting*, 1 (1969), pp. 87-97 (see esp. p. 87).

sum games. (The formal theory of such non-zero-sum games is still relatively underdeveloped, but this is pretty much immaterial for our rather simplistic purposes.)[4] Consider a non-zero-sum game situation of the following sort with two players, X and Y:

X \ Y	y_1	y_2
x_1	2/1	1/2
x_2	1/1	1/1

Here the entry 2/1 in the position corresponding to x_1 and y_1 is to mean: if X plays his first strategy (x_1) and Y his first strategy (y_1), then the result will be a payoff of 2 for X and 1 for Y. And in the other cases the entries in the tabulation have an exactly analogous meaning (so that if X selects x_1 and Y selects y_2 then X gains 1 and Y gains 2). Now in the particular game given, an arbitrator would, if benevolent, insist that X play his first strategy (since this means that *someone* is to be one unit better off than otherwise), but, if impartial, would be indifferent between y_1 and y_2 (since he is regarding it as immaterial whether the extra unit is to go to X or to Y). A conflict situation is drastically altered when the individuals concerned are not "economic men" of the traditional sort actuated by self-interest alone, but rather are in some degree unselfish in making the interest of another a part of their own. Let us consider what may happen when people adopt the social point of view and *internalize* the benefits to another as part of their own benefit. Assume we confront the following game as representing the prima facie conflict situation:

X \ Y	y_1	y_2
x_1	110/60	100/61
x_2	111/50	100/50

4. A major contribution is T. C. Schelling, *The Strategy of Conflict* (Cambridge, Mass., 1963). The prime application of game theory to social situations is due to R. B. Braithwaite, *The Theory of Games as a Tool for the Moral Philosopher*

Here, if the participants make their choices in unwitting independence of one another, the presumptive solution is that X will insist upon x_2 (where he never loses vis-à-vis x_1), and Y will insist upon y_2 (where he never loses vis-à-vis y_1). By absence of communication, they lose the opportunity to realize x_1y_1 where *both* would gain and arrive at what is the worst possible solution for themselves. But now suppose that each valued the advantage to another as a small benefit to himself—say at 10 percent thereof. The resulting derivative game will take the following form:

X \ Y	y_1	y_2
x_1	116/71	106/70
x_2	116/61	105/61

Now the outcome—when there is no communication—is determined through the consideration that both the participants would now prefer their *first* alternative on grounds similar to those considered before, so that x_1y_1 would result. When this is the case, the chances of arriving at a socially more advantageous situation are significantly bettered.

This abstract example puts into vivid relief the significant fact that in conflict-of-interest situations in which the participants are prepared to be at least *somewhat* unselfish—and adopt the social point of view to at least some degree—the prospects of a better realization of the general welfare *must* be improved, an improvement which may well even result also in a better realization of the selfish interests of the parties concerned.

It is noteworthy, however, that the widening concern for the welfare of others, and the corresponding rise of the general welfare on the scale of our social values, has been matched by a correlated shift in the concept of *implementation* of this value. Care for the welfare of others has moved increasingly from the status of a personal concern to that of a responsibility of the state. The heightened emphasis upon the end at issue has been accompanied by a revised

(London, 1963). For a good general account of game theory, with full reference to the contributions importantly relevant to our discussion, such as those by J. Nash and J. C. Harsanyi, see R. D. Luce and H. Raiffa, *Games and Decisions* (New York, 1957).

conception as to the appropriate means of its realization, from personal involvement to vicarious, institutionalized implementation through the instrumentalities of government. (Critics of existing social practices have, of course, not failed to note and disapprove this "let George do it" approach to the implementation of key values.)

It should thus be stressed that "internalization of the welfare of another" can take two forms: (1) *direct*, through caring for it oneself in personal action, and (2) *vicarious*, in undertaking to make provision for it through appropriate third-person instrumentalities. This distinction must be applied consistently in the present discussion. We shall place repeated stress on the increased prominence on the social point of view and the internalization of the general welfare. But throughout we mean this to be understood in its essentially political rather than personal bearing, exactly along the same lines as "charity," which currently involves greater resources than ever before in American life, but is expended through overwhelmingly public agencies and managed vicariously through delegated representatives rather than by personal and direct means. That people will *personally* become more involved with the welfare of others under the conditions of modern life is improbable, indeed counterindicated.[5]

The mechanism of this presumptive increase in emphasis upon social welfare as a personal value deserves at least brief discussion. The general phenomenon of a change in objective environmental conditions bringing in its wake a correlated change in subjective attitudes is familiar: when something grows more important (e.g., heat in a colder climate), we tend to value it more. This is true by and large, but with the general welfare psychological tendencies of a special sort become operative. The deep-rooted sentiments of group solidarity, the sense of justice and fair play, our feelings of sailing in the same boat with our fellows, the empathy toward and sympathy for those about us, and our concern for the well-being of others are established on a local basis within the family, the circle of our friends, and the sphere of the associates of our work or leisure. To be concerned for the welfare of *some* others is part

5. See Bibb Lantaré and J. M. Darley, "Bystander 'Apathy'," *American Scientist*, 57 (1969), pp. 244-68.

of the normal man's ordinary makeup.[6] To prize social welfare as a value is but an extension of this process of making the welfare of others part of our own personal welfare, *internalizing* it by those psychological processes well established in other spheres of a person's interaction with a group.

This internalization of the general welfare of the group as a personal value continues and extends a wider process of social empathy whose general structure is quite familiar. We nowadays marvel that ordinary, well-meaning people in the eighteenth century could be so thick-skinned as to attend public executions in the spirit of a circus performance, without recoiling from what to us is a virtually unbearable spectacle of human anguish and suffering. Again, we wonder how well-meaning people in the nineteenth century could calmly bear to see about them the noxious effects of personality-destructive mass poverty and privation, and unshrinkingly accept this sometimes as the inevitable results of divine Providence, sometimes as the inexorable consequence of economic law. Our society has by gradual, step-by-step internalization transformed into a threat to *self*-interest most kinds of threats to the physical and economic well-being of other individuals and groups.[7] The concern for the public welfare in general, as it has developed in the twentieth century, is but the latest and most comprehensive manifestation of this general process.

To view the issue from this angle is, though correct, yet in a way misleading. It puts increased concern for social welfare into the perspective of an increasing enlightenment, a growing acquisition of those virtues (unselfishness, concern for others, nonparochi-

---

6. Recognition of this was codified into our earlier distinction of *a person's own* welfare interests into those which are of the first order (i.e., self-oriented) and those of the second order (i.e., other-directed).

7. It deserves remark that a value internalization of the welfare of others is not possible without appropriate shifts in related values and so requires a revision of the value schedule of the person at issue. Some former sources of satisfaction must now be abandoned as improper because they are "antisocial." Think, for example, of the very real satisfactions people derived from those cruel sports and spectacles that put *circenses* next only to *panem*. Or again, think of the genuine satisfactions inherent in enjoyment of the authentically deferent service of others which—under modern conditions—is the exclusive privilege of the high politician and the great magnate.

alism) that are the marks of truly civilized men. But to see the matter from this standpoint alone would be to omit the equally important aspect of self-interest and need. For, as we have stressed, the conditions operative in modern advanced societies confront us with a system of interlinkages in which—because of biomedical and economic interdependencies—the individual cannot achieve his own welfare interests without a correlative realization of those of his fellows. His personal welfare is only to be secured by the individual in an effective and stable way through the realization of arrangements that also support the general welfare. Under current conditions in technologically advanced societies, we are brought back with a vengence to the doctrine of the Stoics of antiquity that due care for the interest of others with whom one coexists in a social context is, in the final analysis, a matter not just of altruism but of enlightened self-interest.[8]

8.   One of the positive aspects of such internalization would be to countervail against the *depersonalization* of life in the conditions of a modern urban environment, which generates via alienation an antisocial lawlessness indifferent, nay, inimical, to the general good. The result is a "flight from responsibility" for the interests of others. In 1967 vandals in New York City smashed over 200,000 school windows and 360,000 public telephones, and did $750,000 worth of damage in the city's parks (data from an article by David Burnham in the *New York Times*, April 20, 1969).

THREE

Social Welfare and Personal Happiness

IT SEEMS a self-evident truism to maintain that the aim of measures for promoting the welfare of people, or for "improving their lot" so to speak, is to make them happier. One speaks of the *social welfare* of a group with a view primarily to the extent to which its members enjoy certain of the generally acknowledged requisites of happiness: health (physical and mental), material prosperity, education, protection against the common hazards of life, and the like. The link between welfare and happiness seems almost tautological—even as an increase in a man's monetary standing improves his condition in point of wealth so an increase in his welfare standing must, it would appear on first thought, improve his condition in point of happiness. Unfortunately, the matter is not actually as simple as all this. The linkage of welfare to happiness is not only more subtle and complex, but—worst of all—more remote. There is, as we shall shortly show, at least one very important factor that can obtrude itself between welfare and happiness and render improvements in the former nugatory for improvements in the latter.

In the context of present purposes, *happiness* should be understood as the sort of *perceived happiness* that is at issue when a person asks himself, "Am I really happy these days?" This clearly involves a mixture of two prime considerations: (1) an assessment of mood patterns, some sort of "averaging" of the state of his psychic

---

This chapter is an expanded version of a lecture on "Social Values and Technological Change" presented at the Centenary Symposium of Loyola University in Chicago, January 7, 1970.

feeling tone of euphoria/dysphoria over the recent past and the predictable future, and (2) an intellectualized appraisal of the conditions and circumstances of his present mode of life with a view to his content or discontent therewith. Both these ingredients—the mood aspect and the appraisal aspect—are essential. The man who, from the angle of intellectual appraisal, finds no basis for discontent (he enjoys splendid health, is affluently circumstanced, has good family relationships, etc.) may possibly still fail to *feel* happy; the man who sees himself as deeply unhappy may yet continue in a euphoric state of "feeling happy" (perhaps even through drink or drugs). It is just here that the root of the difficulty lies.

The substantial improvement that has occurred in the general standard of American life throughout the period after World War II—with which we shall be concerned here—is readily documented. As regards health, the life-expectancy statistics in table 1 tell a seemingly straightforward story.

TABLE 1

Expectation of Life
(*In Years*)

Year	At Birth	White Females at Age 20
1940	62.9	71.4
1945	65.9	72.9
1950	68.2	74.6
1955	69.5	75.9
1960	69.7	76.3
1965	70.2	76.7

SOURCE: The data for this and the ensuing statistical tabulations are derived from the U.S. Bureau of the Census, *Statistical Abstracts of the United States: 1968* (Washington, D. C., 1968). For the present data, see p. 53, table 65. (Gaps in the data have been filled in from U.S. Bureau of the Census, *Historical Statistics of the United States: Colonial Times to 1957* (Washington, D. C., 1960).

In the course of the single generation from 1940 to 1970, the expectation of life of Americans, at birth, has steadily increased from just under sixty-three years to just over seventy years. And other recent gains in this area of health also warrant a more detailed look, as shown in table 2.

TABLE 2
Expectation of Healthy Life at Birth
(*In Years*)

Fiscal Year	Expectation of Life	Expected Bed Disability and Institutionalization During Life	Expectation of Healthy Life
1958	69.5	2.3	67.2
1959	69.6	1.8	67.8
1960	69.7	2.0	67.9
1961	69.9	1.9	68.0
1962	70.2	2.1	68.1
1963	70.0	2.1	67.9
1964	69.9	2.0	67.9
1965	70.2	2.0	68.2
1966	70.2	2.0	68.2

SOURCE: U.S. Department of Health, Education, and Welfare, *Toward a Social Report* (Washington, D. C., 1969), p. 3.

From 1958 to 1966, the average American has added a full year to his expected *healthy* life-span (i.e., the time of expected bed disability or institutionalization).

There has also been, as table 3 indicates, a substantial and steady improvement in the financial status of Americans.

TABLE 3
Per Capita Personal Income
(*In Constant [1958] Dollars*)

1950	$1,810
1955	2,027
1960	2,157
1965	2,542

SOURCE: *Toward a Social Report*, p. 315, table 458.

In the period from 1950 to 1965, the personal real income per capita thus saw an increase in real income of almost one-third (i.e., some 29 percent).

It is also a significant fact that Americans are becoming increasingly better educated, as the school-enrollment figures in table 4 show. Between 1950 and 1965, the percentage of the population between five and thirty-four years of age enrolled in school in-

TABLE 4
School Enrollment

Year	Children and Adults (Ages 5–34)	Adults Only (Ages 20–34)
1950	44.2%	12.9%
1955	50.8	16.9
1960	56.4	20.4
1965	60.4	29.1

SOURCE: *Toward a Social Report*, p. 108, table 150.

creased substantially and the percentage of adults enrolled in educational programs more than doubled. This quantitative increase, moreover, fails to reflect the qualitative solidification in American education in the post-Sputnik era.

Moreover, there has also been a truly dramatic growth since World War II in American public investment in social-welfare measures, as is strikingly brought to light in table 5.

TABLE 5
Social-Welfare Expenditures
Under Public Programs
(*Per Capita in Constant [1958] Dollars*)

1945	$ 88
1950	194
1955	214
1960	277
1965	360

SOURCE: Data adapted from *Toward a Social Report*, p. 267, table 401.

The social-welfare expenditures per capita under public programs, measured in constant (1958) dollars, increased fourfold between 1945 and 1965, doubling in the first five postwar years and doubling again since then.

In the area of health care, there has been a similar dramatic improvement. In 1968, the United States spent $55 billion on health services—amounting to 6.5 percent of the gross national product. At current rates of growth, this amount will read $76 billion in 1972 (some 7.1 percent of the GNP). And not only have circumstances improved with respect to the necessities and basics of life, but they have improved, as shown in table 6, with regard to the luxuries as well.

TABLE 6

Per Capita Consumption Expenditures
(*In Constant [1958] Dollars*)

Year	Recreation	Tobacco	Personal Care
1950	$ 91.40	$35.80	$20.20
1955	93.50	33.10	22.90
1960	98.00	37.50	28.20
1965	122.50	39.10	36.00

SOURCE: Data adapted from *Toward a Social Report*, p. 316, table 461.

In the single decade from 1955 to 1965, the per capita consumption outlay for recreation thus increased by more than one quarter (26 percent), and in the same period per capita consumption of tobacco grew at a modest pace, while per capita spending for personal grooming and care came close to doubling.

Taken together, these statistics bring into focus the steady and significant improvement in the provisions for individual comfort and social welfare that has taken place in the United States since World War II. If the thesis that increased welfare brings increasing happiness was correct, one would certainly expect Americans to be substantially happier today than ever before. This expectation is not realized. In fact, the available evidence all points in the reverse way.

A substantial body of questionnaire data has been completed over the recent years to make possible a survey of trends in the self-evaluated happiness of Americans. Operating with increasing sophistication, various polling organizations have made their rounds asking massive samples of representative Americans to appraise themselves in point of being "very happy," "fairly happy," "not happy," or the usual "don't know." The principal findings are set out in schematic form in table 7.[1] There is doubtless *some* looseness in the comparison of these data collected by somewhat

1. In gathering together the questionnaire data on happiness, I have been greatly aided by an unpublished report by Norman C. Dalkey and Ralph J. Lewis of the RAND Corporation.

TABLE 7

Self-classifications of Americans in Point of Happiness

Year (Organization)	Very Happy	Fairly Happy	Not Happy	Don't Know	"Score"a
1946 (AIPO)	39%	50%	9%	2%	110b
1947 (AIPO)	38	57	4	1	125
1949 (AIPO)	43	44	12	1	106
1957 (SRC)	35	54	11	—	102
1963 (NORC)	32	51	16	—	83
1965 (NORC)	30	53	17	—	79

SOURCES: *1946-1949*: Hazel Erskine, "The Polls: Some Thoughts About Life and People," *Public Opinion Quarterly*, 28, no. 3 (Fall 1964); *1957*: Gerald Gurin, Joseph Veroff, and Sheila Feld, *Americans View Their Mental Health* (New York: Basic Books, 1960), p. 22; *1963, 1965*: Norman M. Bradburn, *The Structure of Psychological Well-Being* (Chicago: Aldine, 1969), chap. 3, table 3.1.
NOTE: This table is compiled from the results of some questionnaire studies conducted by AIPO (American Institute of Public Opinion, Princeton, N. J.–the Gallup Organization), SRC (Survey Research Center, University of Michigan), and NORC (National Opinion Research Center, University of Chicago).
   a. In computing the "Score," we set the following figures: *very happy* = +2, *fairly happy* = +1, *not happy* = –2, and *don't know* = 0.
   b. In the case of the 1946 data, an international comparison is possible:

Country (Organization)	Very Happy	Fairly Happy	Not Happy	No Response	"Score"
USA (AIPO)	39%	50%	9%	2%	110
Great Britain (BIPO)	38	56	6	—	120
Canada (CIPO)	32	55	13	—	93

SOURCE: See Hadley Cantril and Mildred Strunk, *Public Opinion: 1935-1946* (Princeton, N. J., 1951), p. 281.
NOTE: BIPO is the British Institute of Public Opinion, London, and CIPO is the Canadian Institute of Public Opinion, Ottawa.

different procedures by different organizations.[2] But a relatively clear and meaningful picture emerges all the same: around a pretty stable middle group of "fairly happy" people (some 50 ± 5 percent of the respondents), there is, during the 1941-1965 period, an erosion of the initially sizable "very happy" group resulting in a near doubling of the category of those who class themselves "not happy." A definite trend emerges: with the passage of years since World War II, Americans, on balance, perceive themselves to be increasingly less happy.

   2. For example, the Gallup people used "fairly happy" for the middle group, while NORC and SRC used "pretty happy."

The evidence just considered relates to the subjective impression of the people interviewed. But there are also relevant data of a more objective kind that indicate a failure of Americans to achieve a higher plateau of personal happiness in the wake of substantial progress in the area of social welfare. Consider suicide, for example (table 8).

TABLE 8
Suicide Rate
(*Per 100,000 Population per Annum*)

1945	11.2
1950	11.4
1955	10.2
1960	10.6
1965	11.1

SOURCE: *Statistical Abstracts of the United States: 1968*, p. 58, table 73. However, the figure for 1945 derives from the volume for 1949, p. 73, table 80.

The suicide rate per 100,000 population per annum has thus hovered with remarkable stability in the 10.2 to 11.2 region ever since World War II. Moreover, since 1945 a steadily increasing number of Americans are being admitted to mental hospitals and, on the average, are spending an increasingly longer time there (table 9).

TABLE 9
Mental Illness
(*Per 1,000 Population*)

Year	Mental Hospital Admissions	Year-End Mental Hospital Population
1945	1.9	4.56
1950	2.0	4.70
1955	2.2	4.72
1960	2.3	5.50
1965	2.9	5.53

SOURCES: *Admissions: Statistical Abstracts of the United States: 1968*, p. 69, table 91; *Population: ibid.*, p. 74, table 98.

Thus the available evidence, through personal impressions as well as overt indicators, suggests that it would be the very reverse of the truth to claim that the impressive postwar progress in matters of human welfare has been matched by a corresponding advance in human happiness. How is this startling implication to be accounted for?

The desired account can, it would seem, be given in something like the following terms: an individual's assessment of his happiness is a matter of his personal and idiosyncratic perception of the extent to which the conditions and circumstances of his life meet his needs and aspirations. And here we enter the area of *"felt sufficiency"* and *"felt* insufficiency." A person can quite meaningfully say, "I realize full well that, by prevailing standards, I have no good reason to be happy and satisfied with my existing circumstances, but all the same I am perfectly happy and quite contented." Or, on the other hand, he may conceivably (and perhaps more plausibly) say, "I know full well that I have every reason for being happy, but all the same I am extremely discontented and dissatisfied."

In this context one is carried back to the old proportion from the school of Epicurus in antiquity:[3]

$$\text{degree of satisfaction} = \frac{\text{attainment}}{\text{expectation}}$$

The man whose personal vision of happiness calls for yachts and polo ponies will be a malcontent in circumstances many of us would regard as idyllic. He who asks but little may be blissful in humble circumstances. It is all a matter of how high one reaches in terms of one's expectations and aspirations.

3. One of the few empirical case studies I am acquainted with that revolves about this bit of speculative philosophy regarding the relationship between expectation and (probable) achievement is Arnold Thomsen, "Expectation in Relation to Achievement and Happiness," *Journal of Abnormal Social Psychology*, 38 (1943), pp. 58-73. Other related discussions and further references are given in James G. March and H. Simon, *Organizations* (New York, 1950); Richard M. Cyert and James G. March, *A Behavioral Theory of the Firm* (New York, 1963); and T. Costello and S. Zalkind, *Psychology in Administration* (Englewood Cliffs, N.J., 1963), see pt. II, "Needs, Motives, and Goals." It is worth noting that one often finds "aspiration" in place of "expectation" in the denominator of the basic proposition. The difference is important but subtle. The enterprising person may aspire to more than he expects to realize; the all-out optimist may expect to realize more than what he aspires to.

On this basis, it becomes possible to provide a readily intelligible account for the—on first view, startling—phenomenon of increasing discontent in the present era of improving personal prosperity and increasing public care for private welfare. What we are facing is an *escalation of expectations*, a raising of the levels of expectations with correspondingly increased aspirations in the demands that people make upon the circumstances and conditions of their lives. With respect to the requisites of happiness, we are in the midst of a "revolution of rising expectations," a revolution that not only affects the man at the bottom, but operates throughout, to the very "top of the heap."

As our Epicurean proportion shows, when increased expectations outstrip actual attainments—even significantly growing attainments—the result is a net decrease in satisfaction. An important lesson lurks in this finding, to wit, that consideration of only the idiosyncratic happiness of a society's members is a poor measure of its attainments in the area of social welfare. It would only be a good measure in a society whose expectations held fairly constant or, if not that, at least developed in a "realistic" manner, that is, in a gradualistic pattern that did not automatically leap beyond increasing attainments.

This supposition of an escalation of expectations, and correspondingly of aspirations, regarding the requisites of happiness finds striking confirmation in the fact that, despite the impressive signs that people think of themselves as less happy than their predecessors of a generation or so ago, they would be quite unwilling to contemplate a return to what is often referred to—generally somewhat facetiously—as "the good old days." Let us examine this evidence.

The best starting point here is the widely accepted idea that people were happier in the days of yore.[4] Note the following survey-questionnaire findings:

---

4. Of course, judgments of this sort—even about oneself—are notoriously problematic: "It is hard enough to know whether one is happy or unhappy now, and still harder to compare the relative happiness or unhappiness of different times of one's life; the utmost that can be said is that we are fairly happy so long as we are not distinctly aware of being miserable" (Samuel Butler, *The Way of All Flesh*).

Do you think Americans were happier and more contented thirty years ago than they are today? (AIPO, 1939)

Yes	No	No Opinion
61%	23%	16%

Science has made many changes in the way people live today as compared with the way they lived fifty years ago. On the whole, do you think people are happier than they were fifty years ago because of those changes, or not happy? (Roper/Minnesota, 1955)

Happier	Not as Happy	No Difference	No Opinion/ Other
36%	47%	15%	3%

Thinking of life today compared to back when your parents were about your age—do you think people today generally have more to worry about, or that there's not much difference? (Roper/Minnesota, 1963)

More Today	Less Today	No Difference	Don't Know/ No Answer
68%	8%	20%	4%

Do you think the human race is getting better or worse from the standpoint of health? knowledge? moral conduct? faith in religion? inner happiness? peace of mind? (AIPO, 1949)

	Better	Worse	No Difference	No Opinion
Health	73%	18%	6%	3%
Knowledge	82	7	7	4
Moral conduct	21	52	22	6
Faith in religion	33	42	18	7
Inner happiness	21	51	18	10
Peace of mind	17	62	11	10
Peace of mind by education				
College	16	74	6	4
High school	18	63	11	8
Grade school	17	57	13	13

NOTE: For comparable and supporting data see Cantril and Strunk, *Public Opinion: 1935-1946*, p. 280.

Uniformly, the result on such questionnaires has been to maintain time and again (usually by a ratio of 2 to 1 or more) that Americans were happier in the earlier period. Although recognizing the real improvements in the circumstances of life as regards health and knowledge, most of the representative American respondents see themselves as living in days when there is less peace of mind, more to worry about, and correspondingly a decline in the general level of personal happiness.

In the face of such a widespread consensus that Americans were happier a generation or so ago, it would seemingly follow that people would hanker after "the good old days." One would expect to find that many or most people would prefer to have lived in this bygone, happier time. So, indeed, it might well appear. But the actual fact is just the reverse of this expectation:

Do you wish you were living in those days (thirty years ago) rather than now? (AIPO, 1939)

Yes	No	No Opinion
30%	61%	9%

Do you think you would have rather lived during the horse-and-buggy days instead of now? (Roper, 1939)

Yes	No	No Opinion
25%	70%	5%

If you had the choice, would you have preferred to live in the "good old days" rather than in the present period? (Roper/Minnesota, 1956)

Yes	No	Other
15%	57%	29%

These findings are quite typical. Invariably, Americans reject the would-have-lived-then-rather-than-now option by a ratio of better than 2 to 1. What are we to make of this? I think the answer is relatively clear. So emphatic an indication of people's unwillingness to trade their circumstances for those of what they have themselves judged to be happier times suggests that Americans have come *to require more* of life to achieve a given level of happiness.[5] Their view seems to be: "To be sure, given what little people asked of life in those 'simpler' days, what they had was quite sufficient to

---

5. One is put in mind of the biblical dictum, "He who is sated loathes honey, but to one who is hungry everything bitter is sweet" (Proverbs 27:7).

render them happy, or at any rate happier than we are today—we who have more than they. But of course we, with our present expectations, would not be very happy in their shoes."[6] This position makes manifest the phenomenon we have spoken of as an escalation of expectations.

We have noted the impressive signs of improvements in the social welfare status of Americans in the years since World War II. But these welfare gains have—to all appearances—been rendered fruitless for the corresponding augmentation in personal happiness that, seemingly, was "only to be expected." The hard-won victory was apparently spoiled by an escalation of expectations that countervailed against the satisfactions to be gained, transforming the summer of our glory into "the winter of our discontent."

This, then, is a summary of the past situation. But what lies ahead? In contemplating the future much is uncertain, but one thing is sure: as long as the escalation of expectations continues more rapidly than actual improvements, there is a bitter ultimate price to be paid in the hard coin of disillusionment. To raise one's sights and one's demands as to requisites of happiness is to become more of a utopian, to come closer to insisting upon the millennium now. But this, of course, is just not in the cards.

It is a better than plausible supposition that—in the first approximation, at any rate—people's expectations of future improvement (or a future deterioration, for that matter) in the general circumstances of life are largely based upon an intuitive *extrapolation of the current trends and tendencies.*[7] Thus if one is dealing with a course of improvements occurring at a decelerating rate (shown in figure 1)—as we eventually must whenever the phenomenon at issue improves in an asymptotic (and so ultimately limited) manner—then disappointment is pretty well inevitable. For in all such cases, when one faces what an economist might

6. There may, of course, also be an element of dislike of change and fear of the unknown which has us "rather bear those ills we have than fly to others that we know not of."

7. Cf. the empirical evidence in Costello and Zalkind, *Psychology in Administration.*

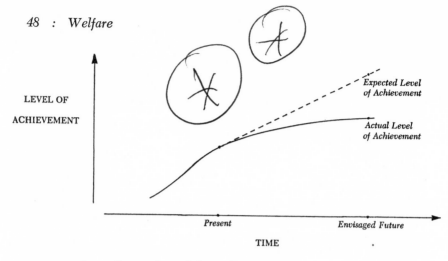

FIGURE 1 : *Expectations of Future Improvement*

call a temporal course of diminishing marginal returns, the simply extrapolated *expected* future levels of achievement must inevitably fall short of the level *actually* attained in the future.

This very situation seems to obtain with regard to many aspects of welfare. As regards improvements in many significant areas of public welfare, we appear to be nearing the proverbial end of the line. Indeed, most of the welfare improvements considered at the outset are subject to a kind of saturation.

First, with regard to the prospects of continuing improvements in general health, it is illuminating to look more closely at the American life-expectancy statistics in table 1. We have seen that in the two decades between 1945 and 1965 the expectation of life at birth increased by more than four years, from just under 66 to just over 70 years. But this seemingly dramatic increase is deceptive, being largely the result of two factors, a decrease in infant mortality and an improvement in the health standards of nonwhite Americans. Thus when one looks at the corresponding figures in table 10 for white adult males one finds that the increase over these same two decades is actually only slightly more than half a year, from a projected life-span of 69.5 years to 70.1 years. These figures reveal that since around 1950 the previous increase in life expectancy has leveled off for American males, despite any contrary impressions based on increases in the general life expectancy (largely due to a decline in infant mortality). Indeed,

TABLE 10
Expectation of Life-span
(*In Years*)

Year	White Males (Age 20)	Nonwhite Males (Age 20)
1945	69.5	62.8
1950	69.5	64.0
1955	70.1	65.5
1960	70.3	65.5
1965	70.1	65.1

SOURCE: *Historical Statistics of the United States: Colonial Times to 1957*, p. 24, series B76-91. Supplemented by *Statistical Abstracts of the United States: 1967*, p. 53, table 61, and the volume for 1968, p. 53, table 66.

over the decade 1958-1968 the expectation of life for American males at age 65 has seen no increase whatsoever.[8] Thus there are substantial indications that—short of a drastic (and perhaps hardly to be expected) biomedical breakthrough—a saturation point is being reached with regard to increases in people's health effective for prolonging in general the life of adults in the United States.[9]

As regards the continuing augmentation of expenditures for public welfare, the statistics in table 11 have their tale to tell.

TABLE 11
Per Capita Expenditure of Resources Upon Welfare

Year	Per Capita Social-Welfare Expenditures (in 1958 Dollars)	Per Capita Personal Income (in 1958 Dollars)	Social-Welfare Expenditures as Percentage of Per Capita Income
1950	$194	$1,810	10.7%
1955	214	2,027	10.6
1960	277	2,157	12.8
1965	360	2,542	14.2

NOTE: These data derive from tabulations in tables 3 and 5.

8. U.S. Department of Health, Education, and Welfare, *Toward a Social Report* (Washington, D.C., 1969), p. 3.

9. Of course, to say this is not to deny the prospect of further advances. As the tables themselves suggest, significant further improvement is possible with respect to nonwhites (i.e., the economically disadvantaged). Also the number of American women who die annually during childbirth puts this country in tenth place among nations in maternal mortality rate (triple the rate of such deaths in first-place Sweden).

It is noteworthy that since 1950 per capita social-welfare expenditures have increased from about 10 to about 15 percent of per capita income. Obviously this trend has neared its saturation level. One cannot expect significant increases in the *proportion* of public expenditures in a country where taxes come to one-third of the gross national product (as of 1969).

It has been estimated reliably that in 1964 Americans committed $31 billion—some 5 percent of the gross national product—to federal antipoverty programs alone.[10] These figures indicate that—regardless of what the actual *need* may be—(real) social-welfare expenditures cannot be expected to be raised very substantially beyond present levels. (Politics, after all, remains "the art of the possible.")

Moreover, we are managing to make no improvements at all in our attempts to reduce certain major causes of unhappiness in the form of the malign vicissitudes and traumas of life, such as crime, accidents, and the collapse of family relationships. Thus consider the distressing statistics in table 12, which shows a seemingly substantial increase in crime rates over a fifteen-year period. In the short period from 1960 to 1965 alone, the rate of crimes of

TABLE 12
Crime Rates
(*Per 100,000 Population*)

Year	Crimes of Violence[a]	Crimes Against Property[b]
1950	115.9	521.8
1955	118.6	626.0
1960	148.3	916.1
1965	184.7	1,249.6

SOURCE: Data for 1960 and 1965 from *Statistical Abstracts of the United States: 1967*, p. 150, table 211. For a vivid picture of contemporary American crime, see *The Challenge of Crime in a Free Society*, a report by the President's Commission on Law Enforcement and Administration of Justice (Washington, D. C., 1967), as well as the *Report of the National Commission on the Causes and Prevention of Violence* (Washington, D. C., 1969).
   a.   Known cases of murder, forcible rape, robbery, and aggravated assault.
   b.   Known cases of burglery, larceny of $50 and over, and auto theft.

10.   National Catholic Coordinating Committee on Economic Opportunity, *The War on Poverty: A Handbook* (September 28, 1964), p. 24.

violence against persons increased by almost 25 percent and property crimes by over 35 percent. And the statistics in table 13 for the first six years of the 1960s are particularly impressive.

TABLE 13
Offenses Known to the Police, 1960–1965
(*Per 100,000 Population*)

Offense	1960	1961	1962	1963	1964	1965
Willful homicide	5.0	4.7	4.5	4.5	4.8	5.1
Forcible rape	9.2	9.0	9.1	9.0	10.7	11.6
Robbery	51.6	50.0	51.1	53.0	58.4	61.4
Aggravated assault	82.5	82.2	84.9	88.6	101.8	106.6
Burglary	465.5	474.9	489.7	527.4	580.4	605.3
Larceny $50 and over	271.4	277.9	296.6	330.9	368.2	393.3
Motor-vehicle theft	179.2	179.9	193.4	212.1	242.0	251.0
Total crimes against persons	148.3	145.9	149.6	155.1	175.7	184.7
Total property crimes	916.1	932.7	979.7	1,070.4	1,190.6	1,249.6

SOURCE: The President's Commission on Law Enforcement and Administration of Justice, *The Challenge of Crime in a Free Society*, p. 24.

The tabulation shows that the rate of motor-vehicle thefts increased by 40 percent during the half decade in view. In 1968 alone, over 800,000 cars were stolen in the United States, an increase of 23 percent over the previous year which itself saw an increase of 17 percent over its predecessor.[11] In the latter 1960s, one in seven Americans fell victim to a reportable crime. (In cities, of course, one's chances are worse still.)

Apace with this quantitative increase in the perpetration of crime, there has been a corresponding increase in the magnitude of loss from theft on the side of its victims, as shown in table 14. During the period from 1950 to 1967, the overall risk of theft per $1,000 of property has come close to doubling. In sum, crime and the fear of crime are significant, negative aspects of life in contemporary America. According to the report of the National Commission on the Causes and Prevention of Violence: "A comparison of reported violent crime rates in this country with those of other modern, stable nations shows the U.S. to be the clear leader. Our

11. Data from M. J. Wilson, "Auto Thefts Being Stripped of Amateurs" (Newsweek News Service Study), *Pittsburgh Press*, November 28, 1969, p. 21.

TABLE 14
Property Loss in Theft (Recovered or Net)
(*Per $1,000 of Appropriate Property*)

Year	Robbery	Burglary	Larceny	Auto Theft	Total
1950	0.10	0.40	0.46	1.16	2.12
1955	0.07	0.43	0.48	1.02	2.00
1960	0.11	0.66	0.54	1.09	2.41
1962	0.09	0.70	0.58	1.18	2.55
1964	0.12	0.94	0.71	1.63	3.35
1966	0.12	0.99	0.73	1.65	3.48
1968 [1967]	0.14	1.18	0.79	1.80	3.91

SOURCE: *Toward a Social Report*, p. 58.

homicide rate is more than twice that of the closest competitor, Finland, and from four of twelve times higher than the rates in a dozen other advanced countries including Japan, Canada, England and Norway." The report goes on to say that the fear of crime, and particularly street crime, "is gnawing at the vitals of urban America."[12]

Again, injuries and death by accidents—and especially automobile accidents—show no signs of any significant abatement (table 15).

TABLE 15
Rate of Death by Accidents
(*Per 100,000 Population*)

Year	All Accidents	Automobile Accidents
1950	60.6	22.5
1955	56.9	22.8
1960	52.3	20.7
1965	58.0	26.5

SOURCE: *Statistical Abstracts of the United States: 1968*, p. 57, table 72.

In 1968, 20 million Americans were injured by pesticides, flammable fabrics, electrical appliances, and other common but haz-

12. Washington, D.C., 1969. The commission, chaired by Dr. Milton S. Eisenhower, was created by President Johnson after the assassinations of Dr. Martin Luther King, Jr., and Sen. Robert F. Kennedy.

ardous products used in and around the house, and some 18,000 of us died of such injuries.[13] All in all, the rate of death by accidents in the United States per 100,000 population has held remarkably steady, about 6 per 10,000 population throughout the postwar period, and there is little chance that this can be brought down as long as automobile-accident fatalities continue their disconcerting growth rate. Nor is the extent to which people suffer nonfatal illnesses and disabilities subsiding in any significant measure. Consider the data in table 16.

TABLE 16
Hospital Admissions
(*Per 100,000 Population*)

Year	Admissions in General and Special Hospitals
1950	109.8
1955	125.4
1960	136.3
1965	145.5

SOURCE. *Statistical Abstracts of the United States: 1968*, p. 69, table 91.

And not only are people more likely to go to the hospital than before, they also tend to *stay* there for longer periods (table 17).

TABLE 17
Short-Term Hospitalization Rate
(*Per 1,000 Population*)

Year	Average Daily Population in Short-Term Hospitals[a]
1950	2.44
1955	2.46
1960	2.64
1965	2.88

SOURCE: Basic data from from *Stastical Abstracts of the United States: 1968*.
a. A short-term hospital is defined as one in which the average stay is less than thirty days.

On the medical side, life prolongation does not tell the whole story as regards happiness. Illness nowadays may be less significant

13. Data from Richard D. Lyons, "Trouble Over Drugs on the Market," *New York Times*, "News of the Week in Review" section, January 4, 1970, p. 5.

as a cause of death, but no less prominent as a source of annoyance, misery, debility, and frustration. The very nourishment in which we seek sustenance is a potential source of danger to us: it has been estimated that last year over 2 million Americans became ill from eating contaminated food.[14] Although Americans *live* longer than in former years, they do not seem to be all that much healthier on a day-to-day basis.

The family has always constituted one of the main purported sources of personal happiness. But here again the statistics underwrite no cheering inferences. The incidence of divorce shown in table 18, for example, has been a remarkably stable phenomenon throughout the postwar period.

TABLE 18
Divorce Rates
(*Per 1,000 Married Females*)

1950	10.3
1955	9.3
1960	9.2
1965	10.6

SOURCE: *Statistical Abstracts of the United States: 1968*, p. 61, table 76.

Moreover, the much-publicized increases of juvenile crime and delinquency (table 19) offer yet another indication of a failure to realize higher levels of family happiness.

TABLE 19
Juvenile Delinquency
(*Arrests in Cities of 2,500 or More*)

Year	Persons Under 18	Total	Juveniles as Percentage of Total
1950	—a	793,671	—
1956	234,474	2,070,794	11.4%
1960	526,905	3,678,836	14.6
1966	1,149,337	5,016,407	22.9

SOURCE: Data from various volumes of *Statistical Abstracts of the United States* (Washington, D. C.): *1952* for 1950, *1957* for 1956, *1962* for 1960, and *1968* for 1966.
NOTE: The increases are in part due to improved reporting practices.
a. Meaningfully comparable data not available.

14. Ibid.

The precise interpretation of all such statistics can, of course, be argued here and there. Statistical evidence in general invites argument. (The increased crime rates may to some extent merely reflect better reportage; the increased hospitalization rates may to some extent be the result of a more extensive resort to hospitalization insurance of various types; and so on.) But a persuasive overall picture emerges all the same. Despite substantial progress with regard to the social welfare, little progress—and perhaps even some retrogress—is being made in bringing about a reduction in the traumas and tragedies of everyday life. Prominent among the principal factors in human happiness are such items as: (1) physical health, (2) mental health, (3) prosperity, (4) personal security in ways other than financial, and (5) family life. The available data show an unqualified improvement with regard to only one of these (item 3). As regards another (item 1), we may very well be nearing the "end of the line" as far as continuing general improvements are concerned. And with respect to the other three (items 2, 4, and 5), there is little ground for speaking of improvement in the sources of personal happiness, since the facts point in a reverse direction. The data we have canvassed thus support rather than contradict the previously given impressionistic indications of a decrease in the general level of happiness among the American people.

However much better off the individual may be in certain limited (albeit unquestionably important) respects, he faces a pattern of life in contemporary society in which the grounds for unhappiness and anxiety are still, as ever, impressively prominent. We are all familiar with other, perhaps less readily quantified, aspects of this phenomenon: the intense and in many ways threatening pace of technological and social change; the depersonalization of life under conditions of urban crowding and congestion; man's pollution and destruction of his natural environment; the ever more strident blare of the media of "communication"; the anxieties of life in the shadow of the atomic sword; the quickening pace of alcoholism and drug dependency; the ever-shifting yet ever-present manifestations of social and economic discrimination and deprivation; the decline in the moral climate and the increase of pornography, venereal disease, and illegitimacy. Substantial improvement in significant sectors of the conditions of life notwithstanding, the potential sources of unhappiness—while here and there removed or diminished—show, on balance, little or no tendency toward abatement.

A larger philosophical issue looms in the background of the empirical considerations we have been canvassing. Can human welfare be improved ad infinitum? Is the Leibnizian vision of an indefinite progress in the human condition a viable view of man's position in this world? Or does the final analysis show all progress to be limited in the final reckoning? There is no escaping the fact that all the improvements in the circumstances of life still leave us with the ultimate reality of the tragic condition of human existence: the frustration of aspiration, illness and mental suffering, the cruelty of man to man, and the haunting transience of human life in the face of the ultimate reality of death.[15] Considerations of this sort place definite and essentially insuperable limits about the kind of meliorism that can realistically be espoused.[16]

Moreover, something akin to a *principle of the conservation of negativity* seems to be operative in human affairs. It is a cruel "fact of life" that the achievement of real progress need not be accompanied by any commensurate satisfaction. And there is nothing perverse about this: it is all very "natural." Man (as we know him in the West) tends to be a creature of discontents—be they divine or otherwise. The imminent goal once achieved, he simply raises his level of expectation and presses onward to the next goal under the goad of renewed dissatisfaction.

One result of this tendency—a result that may properly be viewed as unfortunate—is what might be characterized as the

15. This doubtless largely accounts for the strain of melancholy that runs through the lives of people who "have everything." See, for example, R. R. James, *Rosebery* (New York, 1963), pp. 218, 227-28, regarding the "haunting sense of transience" that clouded the life of this man upon whom kind Fate and smiling Fortune showered every worldly favor.

16. And even if we were unrealistic and postulated a world without illness and aging, would such a world be a utopia or a mess in the face of the enormous social problems that would be entailed? On this score, see Kenneth Boulding's fascinating essay "The Menace of Methuselah," *Journal of the Washington Academy of Sciences* (October 1965).

phenomenon of *hedonic discounting.* This is best explained by an analogy. It is a familiar commonplace that the stock market primarily responds not to the present economic facts but to anticipations of the future. Making present allowance for foreseeable future economic improvements (or declines), the market has already *discounted* them by anticipation when they become a reality, and so underreacts to or even ignores major achievements when they occur. A parallel phenomenon operates in the context of foreseeable improvements in the conditions of human life: a similar undervaluation of realized achievements in the light of prior expectations. Having expected as much (or generally more), we simply refuse to value very real achievements at their own true worth. Once progress is achieved, it becomes discounted as regards its real contribution to happiness: by the time an achievement is made, we have already "raised our sights" in anticipation of its successors.

Now if the escalation of expectations in regard to the requisites of happiness—whose nature and scope we have here endeavored to elucidate—continues, then a tragic time of reckoning lies ahead. The considerations canvassed point to the ironic conclusion that advances have in the past—through their promotion of an escalation of expectations—been self-defeating from the standpoint of promoting happiness: they have brought in their wake a diminution rather than an increase in "the general happiness" of Americans.

Different times bring different situations. Franklin D. Roosevelt's dictum that "we have nothing to fear but fear itself" may have been apposite in the America of the depression. But circumstances are nowadays otherwise, and to a significant extent it is today's optimism that constitutes a threat, not today's pessimism. Danger lurks in an unrealistic confidence in utopian progress that expects that the circumstances of life should every day in every way be getting better and better. There are good grounds for thinking that unless the "revolution of rising expectations" in matters of human welfare is sharply curtailed, a period of increasing disappointment, discontent, and disaffection lies in wait. In more than one way modern technology is a two-edged sword. In particular, technological progress has stimulated a rise in the level of expectations at such a pace that actual achievements, impressive though they are, fall short of expectations. The result here—as always when hoped-for expectations exceed realized achievements—is disappointment and disillusionment.

This era of disillusionment is no remote and distantly prophetic prospect, but a developing reality whose initial phase can already be discerned in its early stages in the domain of current fact. Significant—if not yet substantial—numbers of the most privileged, intelligent, and socially aware among American youth are turning their backs upon a society that has not provided their generation with the millennium. Accepting the facile hedonism and the escalation of expectation that is rife in the society about them, they contrast the idyllic picture painted by such exaggerated expectations with the harsher realities of the actual facts. The result is a kind of social schizophrenia, an inability to accept and to come to grips with the actual environment, marked by the usual symptom of withdrawal ("copping out") and the corresponding tendency toward irrationalism. Wanting to achieve *now* more than is possible, given the state of society and of technology as they actually exist, these young people have increased the trend not merely to impatience but to defeatism regarding man's ability to solve man's problems. The effect is felt in an as yet occasional but nevertheless malign tendency to turn one's back not only upon modern science, but upon rationality itself—to indulge not merely in antiscientism but in unreason as well. Many young Americans are even now traveling down this road in a "flight from reality" into the sphere of drugs and black magic. From an actuality of instant coffee and instant shaving lather they have sprinted on to the fiction of instant happiness (and instant knowledge and wisdom as well). Here is the bitter fruit that grows in the garden of the millennium—that ultimate product of what is not just an escalation but a runaway *inflation* of expectations that must, if the social order is to remain viable, be brought, somehow, under control.[17]

17. The reasonable man does well to preserve some well-known distinctions between his *aspirations* (hopes, dreams, ideals) and his *expectations*: it is important and eminently desirable to "have a dream," but it is no less desirable to acknowledge

The considerations canvassed in this chapter have important implications from the standpoint of social welfare. The promotion of welfare is concerned not with providing for the happiness of people as such, but with increasing the accessibility of certain generally acknowledged *requisites of happiness, so as to bring about improvements in the "climate of life."* Thus—as we have seen—a potential gap remains open between the public welfare and personal happiness. The prospect remains that in a society in which many or most of its members achieve what people in general regard as the basic requisites of happiness, the citizenry may yet by and large fail to be happy. From the present standpoint, it is entirely possible (however seemingly unlikely) that one could improve the quality of people's lives without in fact making them any happier—a prospect particularly acute when people are "unrealistic" in their demands upon life. At any rate (as observed at the outset) the linkage of welfare to happiness is vastly more subtle and complex—and, unfortunately, far more remote—than it seems at first view.

"the facts of life." To have an *aspiration* for improvement, it is, after all, enough merely to be so dissatisfied with the *expectation* for improvement that we must exert knowledge and effort toward its realization.

FOUR

Quality of Life and Social Indicators

THE THEME of "quality of life" has become a focal point in recent public discussions of social-policy issues.[1] One recurrently hears talk of "the growing political necessity in industrialized societies to offer policies that go far beyond the 'welfare state' and deal with the 'quality of life'."[2] In line with such ideas, quality of life is conceived as providing an ultimate and global yardstick for the evaluation of social programs and policies. Yet, as one recent writer has very aptly put it:

The phrase "quality of life" has almost supplanted the older words "happiness" and "welfare" in contemporary discussions of policy in the urban and domestic areas. The phrase does have a fine ring to it and is somewhat less maudlin than "happiness" and somewhat less shop-worn than "welfare." However there is some question whether the brave new phrase is any less vague.[3]

This chapter contains (in much revised and expanded form) material originally presented in an essay "On Quality of Life and the Pursuit of Happiness," RAND Corporation Research Paper P-224 (October 1969).

1. The phrase entered upon its present, meteoric career during the 1964 presidential campaign: "These goals cannot be measured by the size of our bank balances. They can only be measured in the quality of the lives that our people lead" (Remarks of President Lyndon B. Johnson, Madison Square Garden, October 31, 1964).

2. Bertram M. Gross, "Social Systems Accounting" in *Social Indicators*, ed. R. A. Bauer (Cambridge, Mass., 1966), p. 212.

3. Norman C. Dalkey, "Quality of Life," RAND Corporation Paper P-3805 (March 1968).

Here, as so often, *clarification* of the concept is a virtually essential preliminary to any meaningful *application* of it. The most effective way to grapple with the issue of defining "the quality of life" presumably consists in elucidating those specific factors whose presence or absence in varying degrees are the operative issues when questions of a higher or lesser quality of life are mooted.

The "quality of life" has two basic dimensions: the *aristic* and the *hedonic.*[4] The former—as the overtones of the very word *quality* immediately suggest—relates to excellence; the latter relates to satisfactions in general and, in particular, to happiness. The evaluation of a mode or pattern of life turns on two central factors: its *merits* as these are to be assessed by others and its *satisfactions* as these are experienced by the subject himself.[5]

For simplicity let us coalesce all of the felt satisfactions of life under the rubric of happiness. It must be stressed that this is an oversimplification; people may well take satisfaction (quite legitimately) in actions or occurrences which—like Kantian works of duty—do not promote their "happiness" in any ordinary sense of that term. However, subject to this simplifying assumption, we may simply class the factors that augment the quality of life into two principal groups: the excellence-conducive and the happiness-conducive. Correspondingly, in assessing the quality of life one operates with an essentially two-factor criterion.

That the quality of life cannot be assessed in terms of happiness alone is an immediate implication of these rudimentary considerations. It is perfectly conceivable that one individual's state of personal happiness could be higher than another's (other things being equal), notwithstanding the former's lack of education, disinterest in the products of culture and the arts, and disregard of the rights and interests of his fellows. But it would not follow from this hypothesis that the happiness-excelling individual is thereby superior in "quality of life." (We come back to the cutting

4. From the Greek *aristos* ("the best" or "most excellent") and *hēdonē* ("pleasure" or "happiness").

5. Perhaps when the "quality of life" is discussed, the first of these is predominant. In reading discussions of the matter one sometimes gets the impression that the quality of life must be improved even if those affected do not wish for it or enjoy it (at any rate, at first).

edge of J. S. Mill's obiter dictum, "Better to be Socrates dissatisfied than a pig satisfied.")

The factors that relate to excellence in quality of life need not receive much attention here. The few obvious examples adduced above—education, culture, and solicitude for one's fellows—suffice to indicate the kind of thing at issue.[6] But one point must be stressed. The idea of "self-improvement" is both familiar and unproblematic. The aristically oriented notion that there are some things that make us *better* people stands on equal footing with the hedonically oriented notion that there are some things that make us *happier* people. And from the standpoint of individual or social psychology, the former concept is no more inherently intractable than the latter. What is involved in the one is just as disputable as what is involved in the other. Thus if the matter of *happiness* is to be introduced within the pale of serious inquiry, then surely the idea of *excellence* as it figures in the "quality of life" is not to be dismissed as beyond the area of possible investigation, as "unscientific" and merely a matter of subjective taste.[7] Letting these brief remarks suffice as regards the excellence-oriented aspect of the "quality of life," we now turn to its happiness-oriented aspects.

At least three separate issues must be distinguished in any cogent discussion of the happiness of people:

1. *Consensus happiness requisites.* What people in general regard as the essential requisites for a happy life (be it simply for human life as such or life as a member of their own societal environment)

2. *Idiosyncratic happiness factors.* A person's own perception of "what *he* needs" for happiness, and his appraisal of the extent to which he possesses these resources

6. The subject will be resumed at some length in chap. 9.

7. To be sure literary and humanistic spirits are nowadays more emphatic about this line of thought:

> Happiness is not the supreme value. . . . The idea that happiness is the supreme good and the final end has been instilled into man in order to keep him in slavery. Human freedom and dignity forbid us to regard happiness and satisfaction in the light. . . . Man is a free, spiritual and creative being. . . . No law can make him into a creature that prefers happiness to freedom, rest and satisfaction to creativeness. (Nicholas Berdayev, *The Destiny Of Man* [London, 1945], p. 102)

3. *Hedonic mood.* The psychological feeling tone (of a potentially ephemeral character) of "being happy"

The first of these items—the generally recognized happiness requisite—relates to the *interpersonal* sector of the hedonic realm. The list of items that would figure here includes such factors as biomedical well-being; possession of assets[8] and access to services; the quality of the environment (physical, social, and political); status, recognition, and esteem; satisfaction in work-life; freedom to pursue one's interests; availability of leisure; and the like. The above list has to do with what by general agreement the people of a given group by and large require to achieve happiness in their physical and social environment. Which of these specific factors a given group views as comprising the essential requisites for happiness is not a matter for speculative punditry but is a reasonably straightforward matter for empirical—and specifically sociological—inquiry. And this inquiry, of course, would determine not only the items that are to figure on the list, but also their relative weights—what sorts of tradeoffs there are among them, and the like.[9]

The items of our second category—the idiosyncratic happiness factors—are a matter of an individual's own personal view of his needs and aspirations. Here we enter the strictly personal sector and have to do with *the individual's idiosyncratic perception of his own happiness-related needs*: the operative issue is that of what a man thinks *he* needs for happiness and not what people in general think they need for happiness.

8. No doubt the old saw "You can't buy happiness" is correct as far as it goes, but what one certainly *can* buy are changes in one's pattern of life that in one's considered judgment will conduce positively to one's state of happiness. In particular it might be worthwhile to contemplate reactions to some hypothetical scenarios, especially those of an accession-of-assets type. ("If you were unexpectedly to inherit $1,000 [$10,000; $100,000], what would you do with it?") Then one should go on to consider the reasons why this particular mode of investment is selected and inquire into the character of its envisaged satisfactions.

9. Two recent books that discuss these issues and make attempts at inventories of the needs of humans qua humans are P. Kurtz, *Decision and the Condition of Man* (Seattle, Wash., 1965), and T. Clements, *Science and Man* (Springfield, Ill., 1968). Further bibliographies on the subject are presented in both. Unfortunately, the literature of the topic is at once large, amorphous, and indecisive.

Hedonic mood, the third item of our list, is of a quite different order from the preceding two. We here confront something that is simply a matter of feeling, without overt reference to any intellectual apprehension of the satisfaction of needs and desires. What is now at issue is simply a person's psychological feeling tone in point of happiness, his transient state of relative euphoria or dysphoria, of "glowing with satisfaction" or "smoldering with discontent" over the present condition of his life and lot. We now have to do with a (presumably relatively short-term) psychological condition—one that may well be inducible by drugs, alcohol, etc.[10] The difference between happiness as a transient mood and as an ongoing state of things is nicely brought out in a passage from Michael Harrington's classic study of poverty:

Harlem eats, drinks, and dances differently than white America. It looks happier, and sometimes it might be happier, but, as everything else about the ghetto, being poor has a lot to do with it. . . . You will find faces that are often happy but always, even at the moment of bursting joy, haunted. That is what racism has done.[11]

Having been careful to distinguish the three happiness-related considerations, it is only proper to recognize that they are in fact interrelated. The consensus happiness requisites are as they are because of their prominent place among the personal (yet not, thereby, idiosyncratic) happiness factors of virtually all—and literally all "normal"—people. And it is because realization of a person's idiosyncratic happiness requirements is conducive to his attainment of a positive hedonic mood—or at any rate is presumed by him to do so—that the idiosyncratic happiness requisites are as they are. Thus to insist that these factors are significantly distinct is not to deny that they are interrelated, nor to deny that the factor of hedonic mood is perhaps, in the final analysis, the ultimately fundamental element within this range.

10. But in most contexts the question, "Are you happy?" does not relate to the instantaneous mood of the subject but is raised in a broader temporal context that has reference both to retrospective and to prospective considerations. In this regard, "I am now happy," is very much like, "I am now driving from New York to Los Angeles." Neither relates just to the condition of things at the given instantaneous moment.

11. Michael Harrington, The Other America (Baltimore, Md., 1963), pp. 68-72.

Of course, recognition of the fundamentality of hedonic mood is not to claim for it the status of an immediate and primary goal. In this context, the testimony of J. S. Mill is worth noting:

I never, indeed, wavered in the conviction that happiness is the test of all rules of conduct, and the end of life. *But I now thought that this end was only to be attained by not making it the direct end.* Those only are happy (I thought) who have their minds fixed on some object other than their own happiness; on the happiness of others, on the improvement of mankind, even on some art or pursuit, followed not as a means, but as itself an ideal end. Aiming thus at something else, they find happiness by the way. The enjoyments of life (such was now my theory) are sufficient to make it a pleasant thing, when they are taken *en passant*, without being made a principal object. Once make them so, and they are immediately felt to be insufficient. . . . The only chance is to treat, not happiness, but some end external to it, as the purpose of life.[12]

Hedonic mood is the fundamental consideration in the last analysis, not necessarily the first (or second).

We have sorted out the three different issues involved in considering the happiness of people primarily in order to make one key point: that *the consensus happiness requisites are the only part of this happiness complex that is significantly in question in a consideration of the social-policy aspects of the quality of life.* When the concept of quality of life is invoked as a yardstick for the evaluation of social policies and programs, one is certainly not concerned with the vagaries of idiosyncratic "needs" and, possibly, very unrealistic individual expectations. X's addiction to stamp-collecting, Y's devotion to the recreations of the jet set, and Z's longing for vast wealth are pretty much out of the picture. Again, the whole issue of hedonic mood and the matter of a person's transient condition of subjective euphoria or dysphoria is not at issue (or, at any rate, not in the first analysis—nor the second or third for that matter). Rather, the door through which considerations of happiness enter into the "quality of life" as a social issue is provided by the first item of our list: the generally recognized requisites for happiness. The salient fact for our present purposes is that it is the interpersonal and not the personally idiosyncratic

12. John Stuart Mill, *Autobiography*, 7th ed. (London, 1882), p. 142.

sector of the concept that is germane to the issue of the quality of life as a standard of social programs and public policies.[13]

If this view—that the sociopolitically relevant aspect of happiness relates primarily to its interpersonal rather than subjective aspect—is correct, then certain benign consequences follow. It is then feasible to put aside the vast plethora of individual difference and diversity and focus upon the smaller and more orderly sector of needs, interests, requisites, and aspirations that are commonly recognized within the society and enjoy something of a universal status. People's well-being in its interpersonal aspects is the issue in dealing with the social-policy ramifications of quality of life. Our attention is directed not at the atomistic or microscopic level of the characteristics of this or that individual life but at the molar or macroscopic level of the *climate of life* in general.

When considering the quality of life in a society, it is, of course, the individual who is basic. The quality of individual lives provides not only the starting point but also the ultimate terminus of the discussion. Given the pattern of life in Western societies, many individuals do—and all perhaps should—take occasional stock of themselves and their lives, and cast up some sort of subjective personal account to balance the sources of happiness, satisfaction, and contentment against those of unhappiness, dissatisfaction, and discontent. This stocktaking is obviously a matter not of introspecting one's transient state of euphoria/dysphoria but of the rational assessment of reflection "in a cool hour" (as Joseph Butler puts it) regarding the nature, the extent, and the sources of one's satisfactions and their reverse. There is a long list of outstanding people who are on record as concurring in the view of Immanual Kant, who insisted in complete seriousness that he would under no circumstances be willing to live his life over again

13. This way of putting the matter commits some oversimplification. The proper contrast is a matter of degree and not one of kind, as the opposition personal/idiosyncratic versus social/group concensus would suggest. A pluralistic society, after all, comprises highly differentiated subgroupings, with substantially variant conceptions of "group welfare." The critical point, however, is that considerations regarding such subgroups are still group-involving and, as such, contrast with the personal and idiosyncratic.

just as it were. Obviously, a society in which many or most people take this position is not one whose general quality of life has attained a satisfactory level.

One almost immediate consequence of the preceding considerations is that the criteria of satisfactions an individual deploys in the rational assessment of his condition in point of happiness involve reference to two sorts of factors: those idiosyncratic to himself and those which represent the consensus of his environing group. Those items that represent such consensus happiness requisites—health, adequate means, access to personal services, leisure, satisfying interpersonal relations, etc.—comprise the yardsticks by which a broader than personal accounting of the climate of life becomes possible. The coalescing of these factors generates a social dimension of the quality of life. It is only because the quality of life has this social dimension, the *climate* of life, that a reference to the quality of life becomes a workable measure for the evaluation of public policies and programs. If each individual were an atomistically separate unit, a Leibnizian monad, or world unto himself as far as the grounds of his satisfactions (contentment, happiness) were concerned, then the design of socially workable measures for the evaluation of programs and policies would be a task of nearly hopeless complexity. As it is, however, *social accounting*—reckoning up the extent to which the climate of life is enhanced or lowered under specific circumstances—is not only desirable but feasible. This is because man lives a substantially generic rather than essentially atomistic life, a fact in the final analysis underwritten by the regularities imposed by man's biomedical makeup and the uniformities imposed by social conditioning. Such uniformities conspire to carve out a significant area for the domain of consensus happiness requisites.

The situation regarding the sphere of sociopolitical concern with the people's happiness is in some ways akin to that of such concern for health. It is not possible in the present dispensation of things in this world for a society to assure that its people are healthy—as long as aging, accident, disease, and just plain human carelessness make bodily malfunction an unavoidable aspect of human life, and even the wealth of Croesus can at best only postpone the inevitable physical dissolution that is an integral part of the human condition. What a society, of course, can do is to provide for its membership certain resources that facilitate the maintenance of a condition of good health on the part of individuals: access to medical care, availability of medical facilities, public-health measures, health-care education, and the like. A society cannot make people healthy, but it can bring to realization certain resources conducive to the promotion of their individual health. Exactly the same is true of happiness. It would not be sensible to regard it as the job of society—acting though mechanisms decreed by its political or-der—to do that, in principle, impossible thing of making people happy. But it is feasible—and in an affluent society not unreason-able—to expect society to forge those instrumentalities and to create those opportunities through which the attainment by indi-viduals of the general happiness requisites is realized and the pursuit of their idiosyncratic happiness requisites is facilitated. The key terms of this contention are "facilitation" and the "creation of opportunities." The society cannot make each of its members happy, but it should facilitate the pursuit of happiness of people in general and afford them opportunities for this pursuit. The generally acknowledged *means* to happiness may lie in Caesar's gift (think of *panem et circenses*), but the gift of happiness itself lies with the gods alone.

The classical liberal-democratic tradition holds the fundamental tenet that the responsibility of the state should not penetrate directly into the lives of its people but should at most affect their lives indirectly by shaping to the general interest the *environment* in which people live (alike political, social, economic, biomedical, aesthetic, etc.). Correspondingly, the state should concern itself with the life a person leads only insofar as this concern is necessary for the socially beneficial control of the *conditions* under which its people live. Obviously, extremely difficult borderline problems will inevitably arise. But this is not the place to pursue further these ramifications of political philosophy. For present purposes the key point is that one cannot move from the area of general happiness requisites as such to the special province of those parts of these requisites that are relevant to public-policy considerations without taking overt and explicit account of the boundaries of the socially actionable.[14]

To develop this line of thought, it is necessary to take a closer look at the range of consensus happiness requisites. It may safely be assumed that a relatively comprehensive list of these requisites would look somewhat as follows:[15]

I. Personal well-being
  A. Basic aspects of
    1. Health
    2. Wealth, prosperity
    3. Security, contentment
    4. Self-esteem, self-respect, self-acceptance

14. For recent discussions of principles useful for locating these boundaries, see Mancur Olson's *Logic of Collective Action* (Cambridge, Mass., 1965), and James M. Buchanan and Gordon Tulloch, *Calculus of Consent* (Ann Arbor, Mich., 1962).

15. It seems worthwhile to compare this listing with comparable desiderata lists by psychologists and sociologists, such as the "life goal inventory" devised by the sociologists Charlotte Buhler and William E. Coleman, *Life Goal Inventory*, mimeographed (Los Angeles, Calif., 1964); and see the report by C. Buhler, "The Life Cycle: Structural Determinants in Goalsetting," *Humanistic Psychology*, 6 (1966), pp. 37-52 (cf. p. 47), where twelve factors are developed, as follows:

A. *Need satisfaction*
  1. Necessities of life, pleasure
  2. Love and family
  3. Sex satisfaction, attractiveness
B. *Self-limiting adaptation*
  1. Accepting limitations, caution
  2. Submissiveness
  3. Avoidance of hardships
C. *Creative expansion*
  1. Self-development
  2. Leadership, fame, power
  3. Role in public life
D. *Upholding the internal order*
  1. Moral values
  2. Social values
  3. Having success

Questionnaire studies of the factors conducive to happiness ("Tell in your own words what 'happiness' means to you") produce results such as the 1946 study in table 20.

5. Self-development, education
6. Status, success
II. Satisfactions deriving from interpersonal relations
   A. Based on reciprocity
      1. Family relationships
      2. Love, affection
      3. Sexual fulfillment
      4. Friendship, congeniality
   B. Self-oriented
      1. Self-expression
      2. Leisure
      3. Activity, exercise, recreation, fun
   C. Other-oriented
      1. Social acceptance by others, social equality (esteem, respect)

TABLE 20
Specified Factors in Happiness

Factor	U.S. (AIPO)	U.K. (BIPO)	Canada (CIPO)
1. Contentment; freedom from worry	44%	14%	32%
2. Marriage; family; children	17	33	19
3. Sufficient money	12	12	38
4. Health; physical well-being	16	15	18
5. Success in work; good job	15	14	6
6. Helping others; living a good life	6	5	—
7. Getting along with people; friendship	4	3	7
8. Fun; enjoyment; hobbies	2	6	—
9. Religion	2	1	2
10. Other answers	13	20	22
Totals	131%	123%	144%

SOURCE. These data are taken from Hadley Cantril and Mildred Strunk, *Public Opinion: 1935-1946* (Princeton, N.J., 1951), p. 281. A 1942 survey conducted in a London working-class district in 1941 yielded the following responses to the question of what people thought contributed to their happiness (listed in rank order): security, knowledge, religion, humor/fun, equality, beauty, activity, pleasure, leadership, and politics. See R. D. Gillespie, *Psychological Effects of War on Citizen and Soldier* (New York, 1942). For a general survey of recent studies of happiness, see Erwin W. Fellows, "Happiness: A Survey of Research," *Humanistic Psychology*, 6 (1966), pp. 17-30.
NOTE: Percentages add to more than 100 because some respondents gave more than one answer.

      2. Social concern for others
      3. Positive impact upon others (leadership, power, etc.)
III. Environmental characteristics
    A. Satisfactions deriving from
      1. Freedom and recognition of rights
      2. Respect of the individual and recognition of moral values
      3. Equality and the recognition of social values in general
      4. Privacy
      5. Pleasing or aesthetic surroundings
      6. Satisfactory physical environment

It is clear on the very surface that only *some* of the items of the foregoing list are societally—rather than personally—actionable: only in certain instances is it plausible to impute responsibility for them (wholly or in substantial part) to the society through its political instrumentality, the state. Health, prosperity, freedom in social *modus operandi*, and availability of leisure are factors with respect to whose attainment it can plausibly be argued that state action should facilitate individual effort. But status, love and friendship, self-esteem, and family life—in sum, pretty much the whole gamut of interpersonal social interrelationships—are centrally important happiness-conditioning areas into which the democratic tradition is justifiably reluctant to see the long gray arm of the state intrude itself.[16] No doubt, these items also qualify as consensus happiness requisites, but they belong to the personal rather than social-welfare sector.

Thus an abbreviation of the preceding tabulation to those consensus happiness requisites that are socially actionable would result in something like the following greatly diminished list:

16. If self-esteem should become nearly impossible for an important minority subgroup due to its social perception by others, with a resulting national backwash of undesirable social consequences, then some state action may be warranted, but only indirectly; for example, with respect to factors—such as the economic—that in turn affect the matters of "image" and "perception." Direct indoctrination under state auspices—or less politely, "thought control"—is a means too dangerous to be deployed even for the achievement of good ends.

1. Health
2. Prosperity and economic well-being
3. Leisure
4. Personal status, security
5. Personal development, education and training
6. Personal freedom and individual opportunity
7. Political freedom and good government
8. Equality
9. Legal rights, justice, and due process
10. Privacy
11. Pleasing or aesthetic surroundings
12. Satisfactory physical environment

This consideration points to the conclusion that *those consensus happiness requisites that are socially actionable and thus belong to the social-welfare sector are the only ones significantly in question in a consideration of the public-policy aspects of the quality of life.* Thus when the topic of the "climate of life" or the "public welfare" is at issue, happiness enters only very indirectly. It comes on the scene through the existence of a domain of consensus happiness requisites falling within the sphere of legitimized action on the part of the society acting through the agency of the state.[17]

The limited sector of the quality-of-life area which we have now isolated is in fact coextensive with the domain of *social indicators.* These are standards for assessing how effectively the society promotes the realization of those specific consensus happiness requisites that its members consider to be socially actionable.[18]

One recent authoritative government document defines *social indicators* as follows:

A social indicator, as the term is used here, may be defined to be a statistic of direct normative interest which facilitates concise, comprehensive, and balanced judgments about the condition of major aspects of

17. It is *this* that we have in mind in speaking about the socially actionable, and *not* "political feasibility" in the face of the constellation of the political forces of the moment.

18. The term "social indicators" appears to have been inspired by the title of the publication called *Economic Indicators,* a concise compendium of economic statistics issued annually by the president's Council of Economic Advisers.

a society. It is in all cases a direct measure of welfare and is subject to the interpretation that, if it changes in the "right" direction, while other things remain equal, things have gotten better, or people are "better off." Thus statistics on the number of doctors or policemen could not be social indicators, whereas figures on health or crime rates could be.[19]

Apart from a specific orientation toward statistical measurability, this conception of the matter as revolving around "making things better" and seeing whether "people are *better off*" squares entirely with the view we have developed.

The starting point for most recent discussions of social indicators has been provided by the list of factors that figured in the report of the presidential Commission on National Goals in the Eisenhower administration.[20] This commission was a nonpartisan group appointed by the president to develop a set of goals for vital areas of our national life. The eleven members of the commission—supported by private funds and having no direct connection with the federal government—utilized the contributions of over 100 leading authorities and specialists in defining the final goals. The objective of this report on goals was to stimulate a continuing discussion and debate among Americans concerned with the quality of life in the nation.

The eleven areas of domestic affairs with respect to which specific goals were developed are:

A. *Status of the individual.* Enhancing personal dignity, promoting maximum development of capabilities, widening the opportunities of individual choice

B. *Individual equality.* Eliminating discrimination on grounds of race, sex, religion, etc.

C. *Democratic progress.* Impuning the quality of public administration at all levels, increasing the collaboration and sharing

19. U.S. Department of Health, Education, and Welfare, *Toward a Social Report* (Washington, D.C., 1969), p. 97. For more discussion of social indicators and for references to the literature, see Bauer, *Social Indicators,* as well as Bertram M. Gross, ed., "Social Goals and Indicators for American Society," *Annals of the American Academy of Political and Social Science,* May and September 1967, and Gross's *The State of the Nation* (London, 1966).

20. Report of the President's Commission on National Goals, *Goals for Americans.* (Englewood Cliffs, N.J., 1960).

of power among the various levels of government, improving the professionalism of state legislatures and local bodies

D. *Education.* Extending the quality and improving the quality of education at all levels

E. *Arts and sciences.* Extending the frontiers of theoretical and applied knowledge, cultivating the arts

F. *Democratic economy.* Maintaining competition and economic decentralization

G. *Economic growth.* Increasing both the quantity and quality of growth, including capital investment in the public sector, maintaining full employment and improving the standard of living. Fostering productive invocation. Providing education for a more capable and flexible work force

H. *Technological change.* Increasing the application of new technologies while guarding the economic security of the work force

I. *Agriculture.* Improving the well-being of the agricultural sector of our economy

J. *Living conditions.* Reversing the "decay" of the cities. Assuring the orderly growth of urban complexes and the availability of environmental amenities

K. *Health and welfare.* Improving the quality and quantity of medical and welfare services. Reducing juvenile delinquency and family breakdown

It is worthwhile to compare the above list of factors with those of the official document, *Toward a Social Report*, prepared under the direction of Mancur Olson and issued by the U.S. Department of Health, Education, and Welfare in 1966.[21] The categories at issue in this report are:

21. In a comparative study of the "level of living" in some twenty countries on four continents carried out under the auspices of the United Nations, reference to seven factors was made: nutrition, housing, health, education, leisure and recreation, economic and personal security, and "surplus." The operative statistical indicators are the factors actually used for assessment within these categories (e.g., for *education*, the school-enrollment ratio, the school-completion ratio, and the pupil-teacher ratio). See Jan Drewnowski and Scott Wolff, *The Level of Living Index*, United Nations Research Institute for Social Development, Report no. 4 (Geneva, 1966).

  I. Health
      A. Physical health
      B. Mental illness
  II. Social mobility
      A. Economic opportunity
      B. Educational opportunity
  III. Physical environment
      A. Natural environment
      B. Man-made environment
  IV. Income and poverty
  V. Public order and safety (i.e., physical security)
  VI. Learning, science, and art
  VII. Participation and alienation
      A. Personal freedom
      B. Equality and justice
      C. Family status
      D. Social integration, alienation

This listing can without much difficulty be correlated with the preceding one:

$$I = [K]$$
$$II(A) = [G] + [A] + [H] + [I]$$
$$II(B) = [D] + [A]$$
$$III = [J]$$
$$IV = [G]$$
$$V = [J]$$
$$VI = E$$
$$VII(A) = [A] + [F]$$
$$VII(B) = [B] + [C]$$
$$VII(C) = [A]$$
$$VII(D) = [A] + [B] + [D]$$

NOTE: Brackets mean "in part."

By a coordinated compilation of these two lists, we can obtain the following more comprehensive list as a first approximation to a set of "social indicators" indicative of the quality or rather of the *climate* of life in a given social setting:

1. Public health
2. Public welfare
3. Status of the person[22]
   a. "Dignity" of the individual (cf. 8)
   b. The standard of living (cf. 6)
   c. Economic opportunity (cf. 6)
   d. Educational opportunity (cf. 4)
   e. Social mobility (cf. 8)
   f. Physical security of person and property (cf. 8)
   g. Opportunity of political expression (cf. 9)
   h. Leisure and recreation
4. Education
5. Intellectual and cultural environment
   a. Progress in science and technology
   b. Cultivation of the arts
   c. Cultivation of humanistic study and research
6. Economic environment
   a. Economic productivity of goods and services
   b. Economic innovation and growth
   c. Economic justice in distribution (cf. 2 and 3b)
   d. Economic democracy and diversity
7. Physical environment
   a. Man-made environment (housing, streets, etc.)
   b. Natural environment (parks, roads, etc.)
   c. The aesthetic dimension
8. Social environment
   a. Individual rights, individual equality, and social justice
   b. Social integration
   c. Social mobility
   d. Public order and public safety
9. Political environment
   a. Individual rights and freedoms and legal justice
   b. Democratic process

---

22. Note that this factor comes into the picture only through the environmental factors listed under it.

It is clear that these nine categories of social indicators are readily aligned with the previously given list of some of the principal socially actionable consensus happiness requisites (see page 72):

1. Health (1)
2. Prosperity and economic well-being (3a-c, 6)
3. Leisure (3b, 6c)
4. Personal status, security (8, 3f, 2)
5. Personal development, education and training (3d, 4, 5)
6. Personal freedom and individual opportunity (3c-e, 3g, 6d, 8a, 9a)
7. Political freedom and good government (3g)
8. Equality (8a)
9. Legal rights, justice, and due process (8a, 9)
10. Privacy (3f, 8d, 9a)
11. Pleasing or aesthetic surroundings (7)
12. Satisfactory physical environment (7)

Thus even a cursory analysis shows how the area of social indicators blends into the region of the socially actionable quality-of-life factors with which our present deliberations have been primarily concerned. These two issues—namely, social indicators on the one hand and socially actionable quality-of-life factors on the other— are simply reverse sides of one and the same coin.[23]

In the ensuing chapters we shall not be able to pursue the topic of social indicators across the whole of its vast extent. Rather, we shall focus the consideration of details particularly upon two basic fundamentals, namely, health and the economic aspect; for these two aspects of welfare—the medical and the economic, the improvement of health and the removal of poverty—not only represent the very core of the conception of welfare, but are the pivot points about which the modern welfare state has come to revolve.

---

23. To preserve the plausibility of this point, it is necessary to distinguish the complex factor measured (e.g., health or intelligence) from the specific indices used in its assessment (e.g., life expectancy or intelligence quotients). For one interesting implementation of the idea of social indicators in the course of which the need for preserving this distinction becomes very clear, see J. O. Wilson, *Quality of Life in the United States*, Midwest Research Institute Preprint (Kansas City, Mo., 1968).

FIVE

Health and Welfare

ALTHOUGH AN INTIMATE RELATIONSHIP unquestionably subsists between health and welfare, to go as far as to attempt identification of the two would be to interpret much too literally a metaphor like *salus publica* or "the health of the body politic." In one influential recent book on political philosophy, we read:

> The point of "welfare" is much the same in the three contexts [viz., the "material," the "spiritual," and the "moral"], namely, health and the conditions making for health. . . . "Welfare," it will be recalled, refers to the physical conditions conducive to health and with this in mind it is easy to see why certain kinds of provision are particularly likely to be justified as being "for the general welfare": sanitation, open spaces and recreation grounds, adequate supplies of food (especially for children, whose development depends on a correct diet) and medical care.[1]

This conception of the matter is much too narrow. The passage immediately reveals its author as a Britisher who tends to view welfare in the context of "the welfare state" and thinks of this primarily in terms of the National Health Service. (Along parallel lines an American might well think of "welfare" as primarily meaning "public assistance"—i.e., the state's financial support of the unemployed or unemployable.) There is much more to welfare than its medical aspect.

Although the sphere of health certainly does not exhaust that of human welfare, it is obviously a very important sector thereof. Our own approach to welfare has been from the direction of the

---

1. Brian Barry, *Political Argument* (London, 1968), p. 224.

basic requisites of human well-being, and health is unquestionably a pivotal factor here. In this regard, one recent questionnaire study of an analytically stratified sample of over 2,000 Americans is quite illuminating, as shown in table 21. The much closer correlation be-

TABLE 21
Happiness and Worriment

Self-classification in Point of Happiness	Percentage of Respondents Who Worry "Often" About						
	Health	Growing Old	Money	Getting Ahead	Work	Marriage	Children
Very happy	16%	5%	39%	35%	48%	12%	38%
Pretty happy	22	8	47	34	51	9	36
Not too happy	42	28	58	37	54	14	31

SOURCE: Figures are derived from data given in N. M. Bradburn and D. Caplovitz, *Reports on Happiness* (Chicago, 1965), p. 55, table 2.27.

tween happiness and the health-related items (health and aging) —as contrasted with items related to economic status (money, getting ahead, work) and the family (marriage, children)—that is implicit in these figures is striking.[2] This consideration emphasizes the fact—perhaps obvious enough on general principles—that an extremely close connection obtains between a person's conception of his state of health and his estimate of his personal happiness.

One problem that arises immediately in any discussion of health as a factor in public policy is posed by the question of just exactly what health is.[3] Is it simply the absence of identifiable bodily

2. And it is surely a curious datum here that one's children are an object of worriment whose prominence as such *increases* with self-assessed happiness.

3. For a fascinating discussion of this problem in the light of its social and cultural complexity, see René Dubos, *The Mirage of Health* (New York, 1959). "Health and disease cannot be defined merely in terms of anatomical, physiological, or mental attributes. Their real measure is the ability of the individual to function in a manner acceptable to himself and the group of which he is a part" (p. 45). It is clear, however, that this definition will not do. If the group lives under very unhealthful conditions but knows no better (or is resigned to its fate) then the level of expectations in point of health may be set so low that it could be wrong of him and unreasonable of us to regard a man as healthy simply because he can "function in a manner acceptable to himself and the group of which he is a part." To make health a matter of acceptability is to shipwreck the definition on the reef of the potential unrealism of what people are or are not willing to accept.

maladies and diseases? If so, the man who is enfeebled, but not incapacitated, by deficiencies of diet or lack of sleep would be counted as healthy. Perhaps a certain degree of physical vigor is also to be included? But then what of the man immobilized by grief or worry or some other psychosomatic condition? Or is mental health—and with it adjustment, etc.—also to be included? It is difficult to decide just where to draw the line in defining *health*. There are, after all, numerous and diversified reasons why people seek medical care. Many of these stand apart from the standard goals of cure of illness and life prolongation: the reduction of pain and suffering, the removal of debility, the assuaging of fears regarding future consequences of the illness, the lessening of risk of future illnesses, the repair of disabilities, and the improvement of appearance. Throughout its ramified involvements, health shares with many types of *normalcy* a resistance to precise specifications. Health is not just a matter of physiological condition or of psychological outlook or of ability to function effectively under standard circumstances; it is an intricately complex composite of all these factors. This fact has important repercussions. Above all, it will affect importantly just what is being maintained when one asserts that the state bears the responsibility of care for the health of its members.

For the present, however, let us ignore the complications inherent in the problem of the precise construction to be placed upon the conception of health. Regardless of the precise resolution of this problem, it is unquestionably clear at this juncture of history that a state that assumes responsibility for supporting the welfare of its citizenry can do much to improve the general condition of public health. The tabulation in table 22 affords some concrete indication of this fact.

And there have been corresponding gains in life prolongation, gains which have continued to be substantial even into the most recent period, as shown in table 23. These figures show beyond cavil that significant improvements in public health can and have been attained by increased public expenditures for health-supporting activities.

When health is viewed from this perspective (as an object for

TABLE 22
Infant and Maternal Mortality in the United Kingdom
(*Per 1,000 Live Births*)

Year	Infant Mortality (Under One Year of Age)	Maternal Mortality
1935	60.4	4.61
1940	61.4	3.03
1945	48.8	2.14
1950	31.2	0.93
1955	25.8	0.60
1960	22.4	0.39
1965	19.6	0.32

SOURCE: Central Statistical Office, London, *Annual Abstracts of Statistics*, no. 104 (1967), p. 28, table 26.

TABLE 23
Expectation of Total Life-span in the United Kingdom
(*In Years*)

Year	Males		Females	
	At Birth	At Age 20	At Birth	At Age 20
1950-1952	66.2	69.2	71.2	73.9
1965-1967	68.5	70.8	74.6	76.4

SOURCE: Central Statistical Office, London, *Annual Abstracts of Statistics*, no 104 (1967), p. 30, table 27.

the allocation of social resources), health-supportive expenditures may be seen as an investment in human life. And with life itself, as with other things only to be secured at a price, the economist's question of value arises. What is the value of life and what is the value of its prolongation?[4] In recent years the "human capital" approach to estimate the benefits of disease reduction has come into fashion.[5] In this approach a human being is looked at as a productive asset, one who, through participation in the economy, will generate a stream of earnings through future years.[6] This valu-

4. For a historical review of efforts to calculate the value of human lives, see L. I. Dublin and A. J. Lotka, *The Money Value of a Man* (New York, 1946).
5. See G. S. Becker, *Human Capital* (New York, 1964).
6. See, for example, R. Fein, *The Economics of Mental Illness* (New York, 1958).

ation of a man as a unit of future earning potential lays the ground-work for the cost-benefit analysis of health programs.[7] But one must not become carried away by the attractions of a point of view that introduces a delusory simplicity and precision into inherently complex and emotion-laden issues. In the first place, the "value" one is prepared to attach to a life is no fixed quantity but depends upon our distance from its possessor. Is it our own, that of our wife or children, our friend, our associate or neighbor, or that of a nameless, faceless someone at the other end of the world? Nor, surely, would one want to proceed on economic considerations: the earning power of a male is at present twice that of a female, yet no one would stand ready to pay $60,000 to save a newborn boy infant while drawing the limit at $35,000 for a girl.[8] Neither would it be reasonable for an individual or for a society to base decisions about health expenditures solely or primarily upon cal-culations that address themselves to factors of "human capital." To do so would amount to a monomaniac dedication to economic considerations. Nor yet can it be said simply that good health is worth whatever people are willing to pay for it, since people may be willing to pay too little or too much. (The drug addict falls into the first category, the hypochondriac into the second.) In the af-fairs of individuals and societies alike, we encounter a certain "economy of life" within which the safeguarding of health fits into place alongside other desiderata.

These considerations relate to the relative *share* of the entire "pie" of resources that health care can properly demand in the face of other desiderata. But there is also the even more compelling

7. For a survey of the extremely ingenious methodologies at issue here, see H. H. Hinrichs and G. M. Taylor, *Program Budgeting and Benefit-Cost Analysis* (Pacific Palisades, Calif., 1969). In the United States, programs to provide in-creased medical care to the poor have been the fastest-growing parts of the federal health budget. The authorities have been actuated to this policy not only on its own merits, but as part of a campaign to reduce the incidence of poverty and to diminish its economic and social impact on the rest of society.

8. The expected lifetime earnings, discounted at 4 percent, for infants stand presently at just over $60,000 for males and $34,000 for females. See Dorothy P. Rice, "Estimating the Cost of Illness," U.S. Public Health Service, Division of Medical Care Administration, Health Economics Branch, Public Health Service Publication no. 947-6, *Health Economics Services*, no. 6 (Washington, D.C., 1966).

issue of the *size* of the pie itself. There are definite limits to the extent a state and its citizens can commit resources for the support of health. This point is brought home in table 24 by a consideration

T A B L E 24
Trends in Medical Outlays in the United States
(*In Current Dollars*)

Year	Total National Health Expenditures (in Billions of Dollars)	Percentage of Total GNP	Public Per Capita Medical-Care Expenditures	Percentage of Per Capita GNP	Private Per Capita Medical-Care Expenditures	Percentage of Per Capita Income
1950	$12.9	4.6%	$ 78.20	4.2%	$ 56.38	3.8%
1960	27.0	5.3	139.98	4.3	106.15	4.8
1967	50.7	6.2	231.98	5.8	155.45a	5.0

SOURCE: U.S. Bureau of the Census, *Statistical Abstracts of the United States: 1969* (Washington, D. C., 1969), p. 62, table 79; p. 63, tables 82 and 83; p. 313, table 459.
a. It is perhaps surprising that these expenditures substantially exceed per capita outlays by the central government in Great Britain under the National Health Service. These amounted to £16.13 ($53.56) in 1962 and £27.63 ($76.24) in 1967. Data are from Central Statistical Office, London, *Annual Abstracts of Statistics*, no. 104 (1967), p. 54, table 49. The low per-person cost for complete medical and hospital care under the National Health Service never ceases to astonish Americans. In part, however, the economy is correlated with the relatively lower financial standing of the physician in Great Britain as compared with his American counterpart.

of American private and public outlays in the medical sector since World War II. However, these figures point to a trend that cannot be projected very far. An affluent nation can possibly commit a significantly increasing *amount* of its resources to health care, but it cannot long continue to increase the *proportion* of its public and private wealth expended for this purpose—as America has steadily done over the past generation.[9] The Department of Health, Edu-

9. This point becomes more graphic when viewed from the angle of the indi-

cation, and Welfare foresees spending over $10 billion for the provision of health services; these federal expenditures would be wholly additional to efforts on the local basis of state, county, or city. The object of most of these programs is medical assistance to the poor: in recent years these programs have grown the fastest of all parts of the federal health budget.

But there are limits not only to the quantity of medical services that even a wealthy society can make available to its members, but also to what such services can actually achieve, even if mounted on a vast scale. Consider the data in table 25. As far as

TABLE 25

Expectation of Loss of Time by Hospitalization

Fiscal Year of Birth	Days of Average Annual Hospitalization[a]
1958	12.0
1959	9.5
1960	10.1
1961	9.9
1962	10.1
1963	10.1
1964	10.1
1965	10.1
1966	10.1

SOURCE: U.S. Department of Health, Education, and Welfare, *Toward a Social Report* (Washington, D. C., 1969), p. 3.
a. Days of bed disability and institutionalization to be expected on the average per annum during the life of persons born in the indicated year.

these figures indicate, the recent substantial increases in medical-care expenditures would seem to be matched by little, if any, comparable improvement in actual health. By itself this fact does not go far—bed-disability decline is a meager measure of health improvement. But let us widen the base of information. Consider the

viduals involved. A special report to the president carried out in 1952 showed that a million American families spent 50 percent or more of their total family income on medical care that year, and that some eight million families were in debt on grounds of medical expenses. (See R. Dubos, *Mirage of Health*, pp. 178–79.) Facts of this sort are usually construed as arguing that the state should do much more to help individuals meet medical expenses, but they can also be construed as indicating that the society as a whole is nearing an end to what can be done within available resources. (These two points, of course, are not incompatible.)

statistics in table 26. It would appear that further significant reductions in infant mortality are becoming increasingly difficult to

T A B L E 26
The Reduction of Infant Mortality Rates

Year	Rate of Infant Mortality (Deaths per 1,000 Children Under One Year)	Decline from Previous Decade
1900	162.4	—
1910	131.8	30.6
1920	92.3	39.5
1930	69.0	23.3
1940	54.9	14.1
1950	33.0	21.9
1960	27.0	6.0
1970 [actually 1967]	22.3	~6.0

SOURCE: *Statistical Abstracts of the United States: 1969*, p. 55, table 69.

realize. (This is not to say that no further improvement is achievable—after all, it is a somewhat shameful fact that over a dozen countries currently outperform the United States in this regard.)

In turning from birth to death in table 27, we find much the same situation as regards the prolongation of life. Here again the same result ensues: the significant improvement obtained throughout the first half of the twentieth century is being followed by a marked decline in the pace of progress since 1950. (Of course, *some* further improvement is to be expected and hoped for.)[10]

It is particularly interesting in this connection to consider the temporal shift in patterns of the causes of death, shown in table 28. To a significant extent, brief but fatal modes of death have been replaced by ones which are more drawn out, debilitating, and at least mentally more agonizing (if not physically—in view of the intervention of pain-killing drugs).

One ramification of the welfare state's concern for the health of its members merits special emphasis. We may distinguish between the state's *promotive* activities to put people into a better position

10. Fifteen nations or more at present have a longer life expectancy at birth; in the leaders—Holland, Sweden, and Norway—the expectation of life at birth is around 3.5 years longer than in the United States. See U.S. Department of Health, Education, and Welfare, *Toward a Social Report* (Washington, D.C., 1969), p. 6.

TABLE 27

Life-Expectancy Data

(*In Years*)

Year	Expected Total Life-span of Males at Age 20	Increase from Previous Decade	Expected Total Life-span of Females at Age 20	Increase from Previous Decade
1900	62.39	—	64.39	—
1910	62.71	0.32	64.88	0.49
1920	65.60	2.89	66.46	1.58
1930	66.02	0.42	68.52	2.06
1940	67.76	1.74	71.38	2.68
1950	69.52	1.76	74.56	3.18
1960	70.10	0.58	76.20	1.64
1970 [1967]	70.20	0.10	76.90	0.70

SOURCES: *1900-1950*: U.S. Bureau of the Census, *Historical Statistics of the United States: Colonial Times to 1957* (Washington, D.C., 1960), p. 24, series B76-90; *1960*: U.S. Bureau of the Census, *Historical Statistics of the United States: Continuation to 1962* (Washington, D.C., 1965), p. 5, series B76-90; *1967*: *Statistical Abstracts of the United States: 1969*, p. 53, table 67.

TABLE 28

Mortality Rates

(*Deaths per 100,000 Population*)

Year	TB	Diptheria, Whooping Cough, Measles	Cancer	Cardiovascular & Renal Diseases	Influenza, Pneumonia	Gastritis, Duodenitis	Accidents
1900	194.4	65.8	64.0	345.2	202.2	142.7	72.3
1930	71.1	12.9	97.4	414.4	102.5	26.0	53.1
1960	6.1	∼1.0	149.2	521.8	37.3	∼3.0	31.0

SOURCES: *1900, 1930*: *Historical Statistics of the United States: Colonial Times to 1957*, p. 26, series B114-128; *1960*: *Statistical Abstracts of the United States: 1969*, p. 58, table 74.

to handle their ordinary health problems and its *protective* activities to guard against extraordinary hazards. This second dimension of health maintenance is of particular importance in contemporary socioeconomic conditions. The protection of people against the side effects of medication and above all the harmful phenomena of scale such as the pollution of available supplies of air and water (1) must be implemented on a large-scale (usually nationwide) basis, (2) is very costly, and (3) represents no advances toward greater public health but instead rearguard actions fought to ward off potential threats that just did not exist under earlier socio-technological conditions.

It thus appears that even when a very affluent society makes enormous expenditures for health maintenance, there are definite limits to the returns that it can realize: life can be prolonged, but only up to a point; physical suffering, ejected from one door, bides its time and returns through another; accident and malice take their toll in bodily injuries; and as regards psychic malady and anguish in all its forms, the "welfare" state is perhaps not in a much better position than its rivals.

Not only are there certain limits to the health-supportive results that a society can achieve, but there are also limits to what it *ought* to do, or attempt to do, in this area. To some extent this is a matter of how one chooses to construe the scope of "health." But certainly if this is to be construed broadly and taken to include *mental* health, then one should certainly want to draw boundaries to circumscribe the area of what is proper for the state to undertake.

If an ethos of personal liberty and freedom is to be maintained, limits must be drawn about the sphere of paternalistic action by the state to protect public health. There can be no question about the legitimacy of requiring inoculation against communicable diseases or establishing a quarantine in certain cases. The proscription of popular use of non-habit-forming narcotics, alcohol,[11] and cigarettes is probably, if arguably, within the pale. But a state-

---

11. During the prohibition years, the death rate from cirrhosis of the liver was cut in half in the United States. (It was 13.3 in 1910, 7.2 in 1930, 14.1 in 1967.) The abandonment of prohibition was certainly not warranted by its failures to yield significant benefits in the area of public health.

supported and supervised requirement of proper toothbrushing, for example, or similar measures of personal health care—where the health of others is not involved—is hardly to be countenanced. In such cases, it is essential to interpret the state's legitimate role in terms of the crucial distinction that exists between suasion and actual control.

It would appear from the considerations we have adduced that three sorts of limits significantly restrict the range of improvements in the domain of health that can be realized by social action:

1. Limits to what the society *can realistically afford* to spend (not just in money but in *all* of its resources, specifically including the human talents at its disposal)

2. Limits to what the society *can actually achieve* by its expenditures

3. Limits to what the society—working through the instrumentality of the state—*properly ought to do*

Moreover, another quite different sort of limitation must surely also play a substantive role: that of political feasibility. For there are also definite limits—more easily deplored than overcome—to the support that the leadership of a society can muster in terms of human energy, interest, and personal sacrifice toward the achievement of chosen objectives, no matter how intrinsically desirable. The existence of these limits means that health must remain in significant respects a matter of personal concern and personal responsibility even in an affluent and welfare-oriented society.

The aged are particularly vulnerable in point of health; this important issue warrants explicit scrutiny. The issue of personal concern for health is made emphatic in an especially poignant way in the context of aging. From a societal point of view, the prime effect of improvements in the quality and distribution of health services is life prolongation.[12] This leads to the important and disturbing issue of the welfare condition of the aged in its relationship to health.

12. However, from a personal point of view, such things as the alleviation of pain and the remedying of various disabilities (which, while not shortening life, make it infinitely less pleasant) are certainly of profound, and conceivably of equal, importance.

A striking finding of studies of the attitudes and outlook of the aged—in psychological depth analyses and superficial questionnaire studies alike—is that, on the whole, the elderly are significantly less happy than the young. For example, an interview study of over 2,000 Americans recently conducted by Bradburn and associates at NORC (the National Opinion Research Center of the University of Chicago) with regard to self-classification of happiness yielded the results shown in table 29. It is striking here how

TABLE 29
Self-appraisals of Happiness

Age Category	Percentage of Respondents Classifying Themselves as		
	Very Happy	Pretty Happy	Not Too Happy
Under 30	30%	58%	11%
30-39	24	66	10
40-49	25	62	13
50-59	23	59	18
60-69	21	54	24
70 and over	18	52	30

SOURCE: Bradburn and Caplovitz, *Reports on Happiness*, p. 9, table 2.1.

steadily the ranks of the "very happy" decline and those of the "not too happy" grow with increasing age.

The basis for the diminished happiness of older people is not hard to find. A helpful key is provided in the NORC interviews of over 2,000 Americans with a view to the determination of the main object of their worries. The results are shown in table 30.

These figures bring out in a strikingly emphatic way the fact that the worries of the aged focus upon the health-related area: one's worsening health; the process of aging itself, the progress of which threatens health further; and the growing proximity of impending death. With sources of human worriment in other categories, age seems either to bring an objective improvement or else (perhaps more likely) simply to crowd these other worries aside obscuring them as sources of concern by the increased prominence of the health factor.

Juxtaposed with the preceding indication of the decreased happiness of the aged, this tabulation strongly suggests that declining

TABLE 30

Objects of Worry

Source of Worry	Percentage Who "Worry Often" About the Items at Issue	
	Persons Younger than 50	Persons 50 Years and Over
1. Health related		
a. Growing old	4%	18%
b. Health	13	30
c. Death	4	12
2. Work or Money related		
a. Work	57	44
b. Getting ahead	35	24
c. Money	52	42
3. Family related		
a. Marriage	15	5
b. Children	51	15
4. Social-context related		
a. Personal enemies	11	7

SOURCE: Adapted from Bradburn and Caplovitz, *Reports on Happiness*, p. 52.

health and the concomitant shortening of life expectancy represent the principal factors in accounting for the lessened happiness of the aged. As long as aging and death are part of the human condition at all, this state of things is inevitable; the health-corrosive effects of aging can be postponed by a society's improvement of health-supportive measures but can never be avoided altogether. Faced squarely, the plain fact is that there are crucial aspects of welfare, specifically those connected with aging—physical decline and death—in the face of which the welfare state is, in effect, impotent. In a real sense, the aged are exiles from the welfare state: their primary malady—aging itself—is one the state cannot cure, regardless of the extent of its goodwill and the magnitude of its means. To the young, a welfare state can offer hopeful prospects, to the mature it can afford some measure of security, to the aged it can offer but little that counts. (To whatever extent feasible, that little should surely be forthcoming!)

One point must be made in this connection. The welfare state claims to benefit the aged and to protect their welfare interests by encouraging and facilitating their retirement at age sixty-five, or before, as is often maintained to be desirable. No policy could be more ill-advised and wrongheaded than a cast-iron rule of mandatory retirement at this age. (*Optional* retirement is quite another matter.) In the first place, the retirement age limit of sixty-five is a heritage—stable over the generations—from a time when this age (considering recent improvements in diet, health care, etc.) was much closer in physiological terms to a current age of seventy-five or eighty.[13] Moreover, there is good reason (in terms of statistical evidence) to think that people live healthier and more effective lives when they continue in harness, rather than being separated at some artificial cutoff point from a pattern of lifework to which they have become accustomed over decades. (Think of such effective septuagenarians as de Gaulle and Adenauer.) Finally, in a work-oriented society, retirement is often not a benefit but a deprivation—even in point of health. For health, as indicated above, is in significant part a matter of perception by self and expectation by others.[14] No wonder then that people "put to pasture" in retirement often go into decline. The rosy picture of retirement as a boon to the aging that opens up for them idyllic prospects of relaxation, comfort, and rewarding leisure is in large measure a sham and a fraud.

13. Cf. R. M. Titmuss, *Essays on "The Welfare State"* (New Haven, Conn., 1959), pp. 25–26.

14. Interesting data on this theme are given in a dispatch entitled "Soviet Finds Continued Employment After Retirement Age Helps Prolong Life," published in the *New York Times*, February 22, 1970, p. 2. One authority quoted attributes the extraordinary longevity in the Caucasus region in part to a social pattern in which "the psychological aspect of feeling needed by family and neighbors" is especially prominent.

SIX

Poverty

POVERTY HAS ALWAYS BEEN REGARDED as constituting—along with war and disease—one of the principal roadblocks to human welfare. The person who lives in poverty and is *impoverished* is presumably a *pauper*, in the dictionary sense of this term "a poor person: a person destitute of property or means of livelihood; one who has no means, or who is dependent on the charity of others."[1] To be in poverty is thus to exist in that miserably unfortunate condition in which one's means and resources are insufficient to make possible a satisfactory provision for one's own livelihood, a circumstance that obviously poses a dire impediment to one's welfare.

The extent of poverty is incontestably important as a key indicator of how the welfare of a person fares in a society. To be sure, poverty—important though it is—is but one element among others in the sphere of social welfare: no balanced discussion of the matter can lose sight of the fact that as regards welfare poverty is only part of a complex. One recent writer has given a trenchant statement of this point:

Poverty, in the present context, refers to an insufficiency of material goods and services. Though our concern is with economic poverty, it is useful to remember that man can be poor in other ways as well, e.g., "spiritually impoverished," "morally bankrupt," "poor in health." Let no one imagine that the elimination of economic poverty will usher in an era of universal happiness and contentment. The annual toll of alcoholics, suicides, and psychotics is drawn from all walks of economic

---

1. The *Oxford English Dictionary*, s.v. "pauper."

life. This should not serve as an excuse for complacency, but simply as a caution against the notion that poverty is the cause of all man's ills.[2]

This quotation furthermore provides an extremely useful reminder that poverty in the broadest sense of the word has dimensions other than the strictly economic aspect with which we are nowadays primarily concerned: there can be social, cultural, educational, moral, and spiritual impoverishment, as well as the economic. It is doubtless true that the poor have ever been with us. Yet there is one critical respect in which the very nature of poverty has changed over the centuries. In the distant past poverty connoted servitude. The old German proverbs, "Poverty is the rich man's cow" and "Poverty is the hand and foot of wealth," point to a time when the poor formed the servile heap comprising the lowest stratum of a stable social order, when being a poor person was not a matter of comparative economic circumstance but a social condition. In medieval Germanic legal terminology, the *arme liute* ("poor people") constituted an element in the structural makeup of a society; poverty represented a social "estate" not a private circumstance of individuals.[3]

Around the turn of the present century in an environment of rampant industrialization, poverty carried strong connotations of weakness of character. R. M. Titmuss has commented upon the extent to which this outlook characterized the British Old Age Pensions Act of 1908:

If poverty was a mark of waywardness then the poor needed moral condemnation or rewarding; as the . . . Act . . . set out to apply in separating the worthy from the unworthy poor by withholding pensions from those "who had habitually failed to work according to ability and need and those who had failed to save money regularly." If poverty was a matter of ignorance then it was the moral duty of one class in society to teach another class how to live, and to lead them through sanitation, soap and thrift to a better station in life.[4]

2. Victor R. Fuchs, "Toward a Theory of Poverty," in *The Concept of Poverty*, ed. U.S. Chamber of Commerce, Task Force on Economic Growth and Opportunity (Washington, D.C., 1965), pp. 72-73.

3. See the article by E. J. Hobsbawm in the *International Encyclopedia of the Social Sciences*, s.v. "poverty."

4. Quoted from Melvin Richter, *T. H. Green: The Politics of Conscience* (London, 1964), p. 297.

Pioneering surveys of the actual condition of the poor—such as Charles Booth's *Life and Labour of the People in London* (1889–1891), and Benjamin Rowntree's *Poverty: A Study of Town Life* (1901)—contributed importantly to this change in attitudes by documenting the extent of poverty and the character of its causes and effects.[5] But only in the wake of the economic disasters of World War I did the view of the poor as shiftless ne'er-do-wells go into decline. Gradually it became the commonly accepted outlook that poverty is ultimately a matter of social and economic conditions rather than slackness, laziness, irresponsibility, or some such personal failing.

The key idea operative in the definition of poverty is clearly that of *a sufficiency of means for livelihood.* But just how is this conception of a "sufficient livelihood" to be understood? This pivotal issue must be resolved before any meaningful discussion of poverty is possible. In reflecting upon the conception of a "sufficient livelihood," one soon comes to realize that (at least) two quite different things are at issue here:

1. Sufficiency to live at a *minimal* level of SUBSISTENCE or life maintenance, a level of bare survival, calling for the minima of food, shelter, clothing, and medical attention needed to live a biomedically viable existence

2. Sufficiency to live at a *basic* level of COMFORT or life adequacy, a level calling for an adequate share of "the good things in life"—as these are understood within the context of one's socioeconomic environment—needed to live a tolerably comfortable existence[6]

5. Charles Booth et al., *Life and Labour of the People in London*, 17 vols. (London, 1889–1891), and Benjamin S. Rowntree, *Poverty: A Study of Town Life* (London, 1901).
6. The underlying scheme of classification here would look as follows:

    A. Absolute sufficiency (biomedical)
    B. Comparative sufficiency
        1. *Personally idiosyncratic*: relative to personal expectations and aspirations
        2. *Social*: relative to the general standards of the group

Here A corresponds to 1 and B2 to 2. The subjective sufficiency of B1 falls beside the point of present purpose.

Anyone who fails to achieve a level of the first type suffers an *absolute* deprivation or insufficiency; he is condemned to live in a fashion that is inadequate from a *biomedical* point of view, lacking the means to sustain life itself properly. By contrast, the person who fails to achieve a level of the second type may suffer only a *relative* deprivation or insufficiency; he is constrained to live in a fashion that is inadequate from a *social* point of view, lacking the things that people in his environment by and large have. For precision it might be useful to reserve the (now technical) term *want* for the first type of insufficiency and the term *underprivilege* for the second.

To draw this distinction between two levels of sufficiency of livelihood is not to claim that either of them is clearcut. It is obvious that adequate comfort is an imprecise and flexible notion, and it may be less clear but is true all the same that adequate subsistence is also. The point was well put by an authority on poverty writing over two generations ago:

The necessities for maintaining physical efficiency are very different from those essential to mere living. A Hottentot, a Lazzarone, or a vagrant may live well enough on little or nothing, because he does not spend himself. The modern workman demands a far higher standard of living in order to keep pace with intense industrial life. Physical efficiency, not mere existence, is to him *vital*. . . . To continue in poverty for any long period means in the end the loss of the power of doing work.[7]

Insofar as subsistence is itself no absolute, but a condition that can be realized at varying levels of vigor, energy, and "efficiency," the idea of a *subsistence level* comes to be stripped of its seeming precision and exactitude.

Be these complexities as they may, the fact remains that the poverty of *absolute* deprivation and the poverty of *comparative* (or *relative*) deprivation are very different matters.[8] The former

7. Robert Hunter, *Poverty* (New York, 1905), pp. 6-7.
8. With greater eloquence than clarity, one recent authority writes:

Poverty should be defined in terms of those who are denied the minimal levels of health, housing, food, and education that our present stage of scientific knowledge specifies as necessary for life as it is now lived in the United States.
 Poverty should be defined psychologically in terms of those whose place in

(i.e., want) poses primarily biomedical issues of a rather stable kind. But the latter (i.e., underprivilege) is something that can be dramatically varying and shifting; it is a comparative condition relative to that of others and may vary drastically with the general economic level of the environment. Yet not infrequently the two modes of poverty are run together. Thus one early authority on poverty wrote:

The vast increase of productive power owned by modern societies is yet used so wastefully that in London today one-third of the population are estimated to be living in chronic poverty, unable to satisfy properly the prime needs of animal life, and owning no appreciable share of the vast social inheritance which the progress of the last century and a half has won for our nation.[9]

But this way of putting the matter is heedless of important distinctions. Clearly, satisfaction of the prime needs of animal life and enjoyment of an appreciable share of the vast social inheritance of an industrialized society are two very different things indeed.

In the American context, at any rate, a substantially applicable concept of poverty must be construed along the relativistic lines of underprivilege. In terms of gross national income per person or any applicable measure of the availability of goods and services, the United States outranks its nearest competitors in Europe and North America and outdistances the nations of the underdeveloped world by several orders of magnitude. The signs of material affluence are everywhere: Americans own over 60 million automobiles, 95 percent of American households have a television set, and over 60 percent of American families own their own homes.[10] Even the poorest persons in so wealthy a society are in many ways better

the society is such that they are internal exiles who, almost inevitably, develop attitudes of defeat and pessimism and who are therefore excluded from taking advantage of new opportunities.

Poverty should be defined absolutely, in terms of what man and society could be. As long as America is less than its potential, the nation as a whole is impoverished by that fact. As long as there is the other America, we are, all of us, poorer because of it. (Michael Harrington, *The Other America* [Baltimore, Md., 1963], p. 175)

9. J. A. Hobson, *The Social Problem* (New York, 1901), p. 12.

10. For these and related data, see U.S. Department of Health, Education, and Welfare, *Toward A Social Report* (Washington, D.C., 1969), p. 42.

circumstanced than the middle strata of very poor societies. American poverty is not to be equated with poverty in poorer nations—a fact that does not prevent its being *poverty* all the same.[11]

Thus in our economy of abundance the very terms of reference in such discussions have undergone a qualitative change, because the traditional concept of a "living wage" has been transformed, having undergone substantial escalation. For example, a "living wage" is nowadays construed to include not only the minima of food, clothing, and shelter—in respect to each of which there has also been escalation—but also entirely new means for protection against the normal hazards of life, such as insurance against illness and accidents. The "living" at issue here is no longer to be taken as *mere* living, as bare survival, but is to be construed in terms of some measure of "the good life." The idea of the living-wage conception of an economic floor has become tied to our concept of a rising standard of living and has, in consequence, undergone substantial escalation.

How many Americans are poor? This question is obviously inseparable from the question of how the number of those in poverty is to be determined. And this in turn leads back to the even more fundamental issue of just exactly how *poverty* is to be construed.

In considering these issues, we may begin with three basic data:

1. In his second inaugural, President Roosevelt characterized a third of the Americans of 1935–1936 as living in poverty: "I see millions lacking the means to buy the products of farm and factory

---

11. Compare Michael Harrington's observation:

In the nineteenth century, conservatives in England used to argue against reform on the grounds that the British worker of the time had a longer life expectancy than medieval nobleman. This is to say that a definition of poverty is, to a considerable extent, a historically conditioned matter. Indeed, if one wanted to play with figures, it would be possible to prove that there are no poor people in the United States, or at least only a few whose plight is as desperate as that of masses in Hong Kong. There is starvation in American society, but it is not a pervasive social problem as it is in some of the newly independent nations. There are still Americans who literally die in the streets, but their numbers are comparatively small. . . . [But] our standards of decency, of what a truly human life requires, change, and they should. (*The Other America*, p. 173)

and by their poverty denying work and productiveness to many other millions. I see one-third of a nation ill-housed, ill-clad, ill-nourished."[12]

2. In his celebrated book on American poverty, Michael Harrington estimated that in the mid-1950s there were 40 to 50 million poor in the United States.[13] Since the total population was then in the neighborhood of 175 million,[14] this means that the judgment of this authority placed some 25 to 30 percent of Americans in a state of poverty as inhabitants of "the other America."

3. In his economic report of 1964, President Kennedy spoke of the need "to lift this fifth of our nation above the poverty line."[15]

Thus these authoritative discussions of the incidence of poverty in the United States give the following picture:

Year	Estimated Percentage of Americans Living in Poverty
1935–1936	33 1/3%
1955	25-30
1964	20

These figures present basic facts that must be reckoned with in any adequate analysis of American poverty.

Clearly it is not an *absolute* concept of deprivation or want—based on a temporally stable concept of biologically minimal life support—that is at issue in these reports. To see this, it suffices to consider the statistics in table 31. These figures indicate that if we were to define poverty in terms of a *fixed* level of income (adjusted, of course, to allow for changes in the purchasing power of money) and to envisage the determination of poverty in absolute, subsistence-oriented, terms, then the decline of poverty would become far too rapid to square with the reports of its incidence with

12. F. D. Roosevelt, Second Inaugural Address, delivered January 20, 1937.
13. *The Other America*, p. 9.
14. To be more exact, 152 million in 1950, 166 million in 1955, and 181 million in 1960.
15. Quoted in Robert J. Lampman, "Ends and Means in the War Against Poverty," in *Poverty Amid Affluence*, ed. L. Fishman (New Haven and London, 1966) p. 213.

TABLE 31
Percentage of Consuming Units Earning Less than $3,000
(*In Constant [1950] Dollars*)

Year	Unit
1935	36.3%
1940 [1941]	23.5
1945	13.6
1950	15.4
1955 [1956]	8.0
1960	7.0
1965	6.0

SOURCES: *1935-1950*: U.S. Bureau of the Census, *Historical Statistics of the United States: Colonial Times to 1957* (Washington, D.C., 1960), p. 165, series G67-74; *1955-1960*: U.S. Bureau of the Census, *Historical Statistics of the United States: Continuation to 1962* (Washington, D.C., 1965), p. 23, series G67a-74a; *1965*: Estimated.

which we began. It is thus plausible to rule out the prospect of an absolute poverty level as the operative basis behind the reported levels of American poverty.

The idea of poverty operative in these reports is clearly a relative one that determines poverty not in absolute but in contextual terms, in terms of how well (or rather ill) those at the bottom of the economic heap fare as compared with people in general. Now it clearly would be too crude to construe "poverty" solely in terms of where a person falls on the income scale relative to others, so that a person is to count as poor when he belongs to the lowest 5, 10, or 20 percent in terms of income. For on this approach, the poverty rate is simply *constant*. This formula decrees by fiat that the poor are permanently with us; as long as incomes are unequal we should, on this approach, never be able to effect any reduction, or indeed any sort of alteration in the percentage of the poor. The contextual determination of poverty must obviously be done in some more sophisticated way than this. It would otherwise be senseless to complain, with the author of the Fabian Tract, *Why Are the Many Poor*, of "the majority in poverty" among Englishmen,[16] and it would be utterly futile to entertain the goal of eliminating poverty.

16. *Why Are the Many Poor?* Fabian Tract no. 1 (London, 1884).

The identification of the poor with those at the foot of the economic ladder—say at the bottom 10 percent or 20 percent of wage earners—means that no matter how well-off people are within a given economy, poverty inevitably remains unaffected as long as strict equality is not attained. To identify the poor in strictly comparative terms, simply as those who are significantly less prosperous than others, is to pass off what is in fact egalitarianism in the guise of a war on poverty. This approach confuses not having *enough* (i.e., poverty) with not having *as much as others* (i.e., inequality)—two obviously very different issues. To take this step is to metamorphose envy into need by confusing inequality with deprivation. The fact is that equality of distribution and sufficiency of share are distinct and substantially different aspects of distributive justice.[17] No end save that of confusion is served by confounding the two.

Serious difficulties also affect approaches to characterizing poverty in terms of how well, or rather ill, the poor fare on a proportionate basis in terms of their share in the material wealth relative to others (especially the rich). Consider the statistics in table 32.

T A B L E 32

Share of the Total Income Earned by Consuming Units

Year	Lowest 20 Percent in Earnings	Highest 5 Percent in Earnings
1935	4.1%	23.7%
1940 [1941]	4.1	22.7
1945 [1944]	4.9	17.4
1950	4.8	17.0
1955	4.8	16.8
1960	4.6	16.8
1965	4.5	15.2

SOURCES: LOWEST 20 PERCENT, *1935-1955: Historical Statistics of the United States: Colonial Times to 1957*, p. 166, series G99–117; *1960: Historical Statistics of the United States: Continuation to 1962*, p. 24; *1965:* Estimated. HIGHEST 5 PERCENT, *1935-1945: Historical Statistics of the United States: Colonial Times to 1957*, p. 167, series G131-146; *1950-1965:* U.S. Bureau of the Census, *Statistical Abstracts of the United States: 1968* (Washington, D.C., 1968), p. 324, table 471.

17. See N. Rescher, *Distributive Justice* (New York, 1966), for a detailed consideration of the relevant issues.

As these figures show, the relative share of the poorest earners has remained remarkably constant over the years in the neighborhood of 4.5 percent while that of the richest has inched downward from about 25 percent to around 15 percent over the generation from 1935 to 1965. The basis of any really dramatic decline in the proportion of the poor is clearly not to be located in this picture of snail-paced egalitarianism.[18]

Let us make a fresh start on the problem. We propose now to consider the widely current and familiar idea of a "poverty level" of income, that is, an amount of income so low that it is plausible to suppose that someone earning less than this is poor. If suitable income statistics are given, one can then determine this level by reasoning backward from the specified data on the incidence of poverty. The result would be as follows:

Year	Percentage of Poor (= P)	Income Level Such That P% of All Consuming Units Earned Less	
		(in Current Dollars[a])	(in Constant [1950] Dollars)
1935	33 1/3%	~$ 750	~$1,500
1955	~28	~ 3,000	~ 2,800
1964 [1965]	20	~ 3,400	~ 3,000

SOURCES: *1935-1955: Historical Statistics of the United States: Colonial Times to 1957*, p. 163, series G1-14; *1964:* U.S. Bureau of the Census, *Statistical Abstracts of the United States: 1969* (Washington, D.C., 1969), p. 363, table 474.
  a. In these tabulations "current dollars" mean, of course, *then* current dollars.

This tabulation suggests the pattern of a shifting poverty floor increasing in time (even after allowance has been made for the difference—i.e., decrease—in the purchasing power of money).

It is very illuminating to inject one further element into this pic-

18. Commenting on similar data, Michael Harrington writes:

In 1958 the lowest fifth of families in the United States had 4.7 per cent of total personal income; and the highest fifth, those families with top income, had 45.5 per cent. But even more important than this incredible comparison is the direction that American income distribution took in this period. Between 1935-1936 and 1944, the poor (for the lowest fifth, and more, dwell in the culture of poverty) increased their share of personal income from 4.1 per cent to 4.9 per cent. There was a slow, tortoise-like trend toward bettering the relative position of the neediest citizens of the United States. But in the postwar period, this trend was reversed. In 1958 the poor had less of a share of personal income than they had in 1944. (*The Other America*, p. 179)

ture, namely, the increase in national wealth as reflected in the rise of people's average income:

Year	Percentage of Poor ($= P$)	Corresponding Poverty Floor ($= F$) (in Constant [1950] Dollars)	Mean Income per Consuming Unit (in Constant [1950] Dollars)
1935 [1935-1936]	33 1/3%	~$1,500	$2,937
1955	~28	~ 2,800	5,054
1964 [1965]	20	~ 3,000	6,600

SOURCES: 1935-1955: *Historical Statistics of the United States: Colonial Times to 1957*, p. 166, series 121; *1964*: Estimated on the basis of *Historical Statistics of the United States: Continuation to 1962*, p. 24.

This tabulation brings a striking phenomenon to the fore: *the poverty floor hovers in the neighborhood of half the average income.*[19] It appears that to all intents and purposes one is confronted with a flexible poverty floor, an *escalating* floor that rises proportionally with income. This poverty floor is not fixed so as to reflect an *absolute* conception of poverty, but is a shifting level whose changes are geared to those in the mean income. Thus in the reports on poverty that were the starting point of this analysis, (1) we do not seem to be dealing with an absolute conception of poverty in terms of the ability to afford the basic requisites of survival, and moreover (2) we do not seem to be dealing with a simply comparative conception of poverty that contrasts how well (or rather ill) the poor are faring in contrast to others. Rather (3) we appear to be confronting a *contextual* conception of poverty, articulated in terms of what goods and services the economy *can afford to provide for people* (on the average).

Regardless of the theoretical adequacy of the conception of poverty that we have been seeking to account for the facts cited, the analysis of poverty that underlies this moveable-floor approach

19. After having been led to this criterion of poverty by the line of reasoning set out above, I found the same standard used by Victor R. Fuchs in his paper "Toward a Theory of Poverty." Fuchs adopts this criterion without supporting argument, simply making the remark, "Many other relative standards could be set, but this is not an unreasonable one, and many of the inferences drawn would be valid for other definitions of this type" (p. 74).

yields certain very useful lessons. First, it highlights the fact that in discussing poverty in a modern industrial economy, and certainly in a postindustrial, affluent economy, the operative issue is not merely one of absolute deprivation but one of relative or comparative deprivation. Here it will not be the minimal-subsistence but the basic-comfort concept of poverty that must be borne in mind. Secondly, the present concept of poverty is tied to the idea of a shifting poverty level, of a "poverty floor" that may drop or escalate. (In a very poor, highly underdeveloped economy, poverty may have to assume its minimal, hard-core meaning when "the floor" is at "subsistence" level.) Thirdly, in general this approach relativizes poverty to what the economy can afford under existing circumstances. Impoverishment is thus coordinated with general prosperity and is not in the first analysis comparative to what others have, but only indirectly so. Fourthly, since a relative and comparative concept of poverty is at issue, it is disingenuous to discuss the topic in terms of the rhetoric of absolute privation, subsistence, and the essential necessities of life. An honest approach calls for the rhetoric of distributive justice and a share in the good life. To say this is not to deny that there is, even in prosperous America, a great deal of outright privation of the necessities of life. Needed publicity has rightly been given to the shocking incidence of actual starvation and dire inability to secure, for lack of means, the goods and services required to maintain life above the level of subsistence. But the current plaints over the massive poverty on the scale of many millions cannot, without lack of candor, claim genuine *want* as the real object of concern in these cases; the actual issue is one of comparative underprivilege.

We must explore somewhat further the implications of the concept of poverty that arise when the floor is pegged at a fixed percentage (say 50 percent) of the average (mean or median) income.[20] Consider, to begin with, what this conception of poverty in terms of a floor set by the equation

$$F = \tfrac{1}{2}I$$

20. In the present context, the difference between mean and median is pretty much irrelevant.

(where F represents the floor and I the average income) would imply for the incidence of poverty in America over the years since the Great Depression (see table 33).

TABLE 33
Poverty in America Since the Depression

Year	Median Income per Consuming Unit (I) (in Current Dollars)	I (in Constant [1959] Dollars)	50 Percent of I (in Current Dollars)	Percentage of Consuming Units Earning Less
1935	$1,631[a]	$2,937	$ 815	~35%[c]
1940 [1941]	2,209[a]	3,664[a]	1,104	~30[c]
1945 [1944]	3,614[a]	4,650[a]	1,807	~26[c]
1950	4,444[a]	4,444[a]	2,222	~26[c]
1955	5,640[a]	5,054 [a]	2,820	~25[c]
1960	6,174[b]	~5,550[a]	3,087	~22[d]
1965	7,154[b]	~6,200	3,577	~21[e]

SOURCES: (a) *Historical Statistics of the United States: Colonial Times to 1957*, p. 166, series 120-121. (b) *Statistical Abstracts of the United States: 1968*, p. 325, table 473. (c) *Historical Statistics of the United States: Colonial Times to 1957*, p. 153, series G2-14. (d) *Historical Statistics of the United States: Continuation to 1962*, p. 22. (e) Estimated.

Comparison of these results with our initially considered reports regarding the prevalence of poverty shows a striking degree of agreement:

Year	Reported	Value from Table
1935	33 1/3%	~35
Early 1950s	25-30	~26
1965	20	~21

This close agreement would seem to confirm the suggestion that the notion of "poverty" underlying the reports of its incidence is in fact pegged to the idea of a shifting "poverty floor," definable in terms of income and set at approximately 50 percent of the median or average income. This conception of poverty relative to this income-based floor, $F = \frac{1}{2}I$, squares remarkably well with intuitive appraisals of the level of poverty.[21] One striking feature of this conception of poverty deserves special note: it represents a relative construction of poverty with the result that the eradication of "poverty" becomes a much more difficult task than it would be on an absolute construction of outright want. This feature is forcibly brought to light by the data in table 34. Despite the dramatic reduction of poverty by an absolute stan-

T A B L E 34
Percentage of U.S. Families Classified as Poor by Relative and Absolute Standards, 1947-1960

		Percentage of Families with Income		
Year	Median Income (in 1959 Dollars)	Less than One-half the Median[a]	Less than $3,000 (in 1959 Dollars)	Less than $2,000 (in 1959 Dollars)
1948	$3,868	19.4%	34.7%	19.8%
1950	4,036	20.0	33.0	19.8
1952	4,277	19.0	29.3	17.8
1954	4,530	20.7	28.7	18.1
1956	5,129	19.5	23.6	14.2
1958	5,143	19.9	23.8	14.1
1960	5,547	20.2	22.1	13.2

SOURCE: U.S. Bureau of the Census, *Trends in the Income of Families and Persons in the United States: 1947-1960*, Technical Paper no. 8 (Washington, D.C., 1963), table 1. The table is reprinted in Victor R. Fuchs, "Toward a Theory of Poverty," in *The Concept of Poverty*, ed. U.S. Chamber of Commerce, Task Force on Economic Growth and Opportunity (Washington, D.C., 1965), p. 75.
a. Estimated by interpolation.

21. The formula employed by the president's Council of Economic Advisers in its 1964 Annual Report classified a family unit as "poor" when its money income is less than $3,000 per year and a single person if his income falls below $1,500. In 1964 the average family income was ∼$6,200 and the average individual income was ∼$3,100. These figures, too, agree quite well with our proposed standard of poverty determination.

A word on methodology may be in order. The discussion has attempted to give what philosophers (following R. Carnap) call a "rational reconstruction" of the

dard, poverty in the sense of our criterion has remained relatively constant during the most recent period. (Note that the discrepancy between this result and that in table 33, which indicates a modest decline in poverty over this period, is due to the fact that we are dealing here with families specifically, whereas the former data related to consuming units in general.)

Consider the comparable data for Great Britain in table 35:

TABLE 35
Income Distribution in the United Kingdom

Year	Average (Mean) Income per Income Earner (in Current Pounds)	Percentage of Income Earners Earning Less than Half the Mean Income
1949-1950	£415	~22%
1961	720	~28
1965	830	~30

NOTE: The percentages in column three are calculated by interpolation from distribution of personal income data given in *Whitaker's Almanac, 1953*, p. 590; *1963*, p. 598; and *1967*, p. 620.

The surprising conclusion indicated by these figures is that poverty in the sense of our comparative criterion has actually been increasing in the British welfare state during the postwar era of increasing affluence. This suggests the conclusion (which can also be substantiated from other points of view) that the key thesis of Michael Harrington's book, *The Other America,* namely that the benefits of the welfare state operative in affluent America redound to the middle sector of the socioeconomic area and have tended to bypass the bottom, is applicable to Great Britain as well.

It is also appropriate to analyze some of the theoretical implications of the $F = \frac{1}{2}I$ determination of a poverty floor. On a *static* basis, we obtain a purely distributional concept of poverty. This is made clear by the diagrammatic representation in figure 2. Figure 2 suggests (quite rightly) that the conception of poverty here operative is fundamentally a measure of inequality of distribution toward the lower end of the income scale.

---

concept of poverty. That is, beginning with the somewhat loose and undefined "presystematic" conception that is at work in the general usage, we have sought to provide a precise and exact specification that yields concordant results.

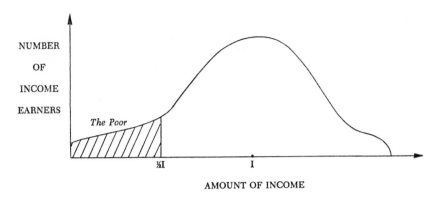

FIGURE 2 : *Distributional Concept of Poverty*

Viewed statically, this concept of poverty points to an aspect of distributive justice: given a sufficiently equitable distribution of the total product earmarked for distribution as income, poverty can be eliminated. Thus consider a population of five persons, with a total income-allocated product of 100 units. Then $I = 20$ and so $\frac{1}{2}I = 10$. Thus if the distribution is 5, 5, 5, 5, 80, then four-fifths of the population is poor (in the sense of our criterion of impoverishment). On the other hand, if the distribution is 15, 15, 15, 25, 30, then there are no poor. (This finding incidentally suggests— I think quite rightly—that the achievement of distributive justice can involve more than merely the eradication of poverty.)

On a *dynamic* basis, the $F = \frac{1}{2}I$ poverty floor points in a *production*-oriented direction, for it ties the level of poverty to a floor F that is readjusted in the light of a rising (or declining) level I of average income. Thus consider again a five-person society with an initial product of 100 units and an initial distribution 9, 9, 16, 16, 50. Here we have a poverty level of 10, leading to a 40 percent incidence of poverty. But if an added 25 units are produced, and equally distributed, we have the income distribution 14, 14, 21, 21, 55. Now $I = 25$, so that $F = 12.5$, and the result is that poverty has been eliminated.

The preceding example shows that it is by no means necessary for elimination of poverty (in the sense now at issue) that the added product should go exclusively to those "at the bottom of the heap." But it is also clear that this would be the distribution of the added product that is maximally *efficient* in the elimination of poverty. Thus consider again a population of five with an initial product of 100 divided as follows: 6, 6, 6, 41, 41. If poverty (in our sense) is to be removed by an added product distributed equally, then the resulting distribution will have the form:

$$6 + x, 6 + x, 6 + x, 41 + x, 41 + x.$$

Now $I = 20 + x$, so that $F = \frac{1}{2}I = 10 + \frac{1}{2}x$. Here, then the least well-off will be lifted above the floor when

$$6 + x \geq 10 + \frac{1}{2}x$$
$$\frac{1}{2}x \geq 4$$
$$x \geq 8.$$

Thus the added product needed to achieve the goal of eliminating poverty, that is, $5x$, must be greater than or equal to 40. Now if the case were different, and the added product were solely to be divided among the poor, then the resulting distribution would have the form

$$6 + y, 6 + y, 6 + y, 41, 41.$$

Now $I = 20 + (3/5)y$, so that $F = \frac{1}{2}I = 10 + (3/10)y$. Here, then, the least well-off will be lifted above the floor when

$$6 + y \geq 10 + (3/10)y$$
$$(7/10)y \geq 4$$
$$y \geq 40/7 = 5.7.$$

Now the added product required to realize the goal of poverty eradication is $3y = 17.1$, so that the added product required is less than half of what it was in the previous case. The lesson—one that is intuitively obvious—is that if other things were equal (which in a real-life economy they are not), the most efficient way of removing poverty without actual redistribution would be to let the added product accrue solely to the poor.

One further implication of the $F = \frac{1}{2}I$ construction of poverty must be mentioned. Clearly at some point of increasing national affluence this entire approach must be abandoned. Once the mean income (and correspondingly ½*I*) grows to very substantial proportions, the applicability of the present construction of *poverty* must be abandoned in favor of some more explicitly comparative concept of relative lack of prosperity. Otherwise, talk of the great prosperity of the poor would no longer be anomalous, and "the rich poor" would cease to be a contradiction in terms. Once *poor* no longer means *needy* (however liberally construed) but just *greedy*, the time to abandon our criterion of poverty is at hand. And correspondingly, remarks would be applicable at the other end of the spectrum, when *I* is too small. It is in the midrange that the criterion is of real value.

In commenting on Michael Harrington's contention that "one cannot raise the bottom of society without benefiting everyone above,"[22] one authority complains that "this is almost precisely wrong. It is probably closer to the truth to say that one cannot raise the bottom except at the expense of those above, and those who are not far removed from the bottom are likely to feel the change most keenly."[23] The examples we have considered show that both claims are wrong, or rather that neither is unqualifiedly correct. A redistributionalistic removal of poverty certainly need not benefit everyone; redirecting resources from the top of the bottom would certainly affect unfavorably those previously near to the bottom, for they then would become a part of the bottom, after having previously been above it.[24]

There is in actual fact a good deal of solid evidence regarding the United States and Britain that as welfare benefits for the poor, and especially the unemployed poor, improve, the near poor, espe-

22. *The Other America*, p. 160.
23. Victor R. Fuchs, "Toward A Theory of Poverty," p. 8-9.
24. And there is another aspect to the matter. Funding the removal of the poverty of specific individuals in the distributive sector of welfare is competitive with the funding of measures in the collective sector for facilities that "benefit everyone alike." Concretely, the money a community must spend on public assistance is not available for creating clearer streets, better schools, improved hospitals, fresher air, and the like. Because of this competition for public funds available for welfare-supportive purposes, measures to remedy poverty may well fail to redound to the *general* benefit. But, of course, those specific poverty-alleviating measures that, by rendering the poor self-supporting, in the end free public funds for other purposes may well ultimately "benefit everyone alike."

cially the workers of the very lowest category, become resentful. They are quite understandably disturbed as welfare benefits approach and sometimes exceed the incomes of men who work at regular, hard, and often dirty or unpleasant jobs. The poor workingman who takes pride in getting by without public assistance cannot but view with dismay the prospect that the nonworking poor, whom he regards with a mixture of contempt and pity, should fare better than he himself in economic terms. Especially galling is the fact that the unemployed are funded by a system of taxation to which he is constrained to contribute.

Thus a redistributionistic attack on poverty can well fail to prove positively beneficial for everyone involved. A productionistic removal of poverty, on the other hand, may well benefit everyone, since it can avoid a degradation in the relative standing of those near the bottom. The removal of poverty as such does not require the one or the other specific route; it is a matter of a choice of programs and policies. If one is serious enough about the goal of removing poverty, one may as well be pragmatic about the means of its attainment. It is then pointless to be doctrinaire about the redistributionistic or the productionistic approach. There is nothing inherent in the desideratum of removing poverty that would force its implementation along one inevitable line.

Yet one other lesson inherent in these considerations deserves added stress. Sometimes poverty is discussed in terms of the rhetoric of hard-core deprivation, at other times in the rhetoric of egalitarianism. Either approach is insufficient because the rhetoric of productivity is also needed. The point is that in the discussion of poverty all of the factors at issue in the sphere of distributive justice must be brought to bear conjointly.

Poverty has been treated in this chapter primarily from the angle of economic statistics. Such statistics unquestionably have a cold, unfeeling look; they present a smooth, hard surface that gives no signs of the pain and misery, the anguish, human suffering, and degradation that lie beneath. Moreover, in dwelling upon the strictly economic side of poverty, there is some tendency to ignore its consequential extraeconomic dimensions in terms of ill health, environmental ugliness, and exclusion from the intellectually, culturally, and aesthetically enriching dimensions of human experience.[25] In taking the economic approach, we certainly have no desire to gloss over the multifaceted baneful aspect of poverty. It is necessary to translate lack of economic means into bad food, ugly housing, noxious surroundings, inadequate medical care, and the manifold other life-conditioning effects of impoverishment.[26] People living in squalor cannot live a full life, and scenes of dire impoverishment are inevitably darkened with the shadows of human tragedy. But the fact is that economics lies at the root of the matter, and it is only by coping with the economic basis of poverty that its eradication can become possible. And this, of course, constitutes a prime social desideratum, since the abolition of poverty would not just redound to the benefit of the poor alone; it could well improve the general climate and quality of life in the society. But to realize this eminently humane objective, the cold, dispassionate analysis of the economic facts of the matter is indispensable. Just as a dangerous illness is not cured by commiseration or sympathy but by medical knowledge, so poverty will not be removed by compassion, or even by "charity," but by the implementation of economic expertise.[27]

One final point: we have spoken of a shifting poverty floor artic-

25. But it is also worth noting that there are other, perhaps no less noxious, modes of impoverishment in its wider sense that do not heavily impact upon the economically poor. Deprivation has many faces, and one of the most dire of them is poverty of social interaction, the shared experiences that make for a sense of belonging and a sense of community with those about one, and whose absence makes for alienation. Such impoverishment of meaningful human fellowship falls less often to the lot of the actually poor than to that of those more fortunately circumstanced.

26. Thus, to take only one example, according to reports of the 1960 census, 15.6 million of the 58,000,000 occupied dwelling units in the United States were substandard. This represented 27 per cent of the nation's total housing supply. Of these, some 3,000,000 were shacks, hovels, and tenements. Another 8.3 million units were "deteriorating," and 4.3 million units were structurally sound but lacking some or all of the essential plumbing facilities. In addition, these figures do not take account of "sound" housing that is terribly overcrowded. (Harrington, *The Other America*, p. 137)

27. Clear popular discussion of economic aspects of poverty is given in Delbert A. Snyder, *Economic Myth and Realty* (Englewood Cliffs, N.J., 1965). An excellent survey of the problem of poverty in America as a whole is presented in B. B. Seligman, ed., *Poverty as a Public Issue* (New York, 1965).

ulated in a contextual way with reference to *what the economy can afford.* This concept, of course, poses large and difficult issues. There are, of course, simple cases: a tribe of aborigines cannot set its members up in retirement at the local Hilton hotel at age sixty. But often the case is less straightforward. It may be quite unclear whether a given economy can afford one or another of the welfare-supportive programs that may be proposed, for the deployment of resources into such programs must compete for resources with other commitments of the society (defense, space exploration, educational programs, etc.). At this point, the *can* of "can afford" shifts from the region of technical feasibility into that of political viability. We shall ultimately have to pursue these political ramifications of the problem in the separate chapter they deserve.[28]

Appendix to Chapter 6

It is of interest to consider the concept of *prosperity* that corresponds to that of *poverty* as laid down in the preceding discussion. If the poor man is one whose income is less than half the average, it seems plausible enough to postulate that the prosperous or affluent man is one whose income exceeds twice the average. We thus arrive at the idea of a prosperity ceiling, a level of affluence—comparable to the level of a poverty floor—defined by the equation:

$$A = 2I.$$

This conception leads to the picture of the development of relative poverty and prosperity in the United States since the time of the Great Depression given in table 36.

Three features of this tabulation are of particular interest: (1) the (increasingly gradual) decline of "poverty" from one-third to one-fifth of the population, (2) the gradual growth of the economic "middle sector" of Americans from one-half of the population to two-thirds, and (3) the rebounding of the prosperous sector which, from a level of around 15 percent in the prewar years, declined to around half this size in the wake of the Second World War but appears in the 1960s to be climbing upward toward its

28. See chap. 8.

T A B L E 36

Poverty and Prosperity in the United States Since the Depression

Year	Median Income (I) per Income Unit (in Current Dollars)[a]	50 Percent of I[a]	Percentage of Units Earning Less[a]	$2 \times I$	Percentage of Units Earning More	Residual Percentage in Neither Category
1935	$1,631	$ 815	~35%	$ 3,262	~15%[b]	~50%
1940 [1941]	2,209	1,104	~30	4,418	~13[b]	~57
1945 [1944]	3,614	1,807	~26	7,218	~8.5[b]	~65.5
1950	4,444	2,222	~26	8,888	~7.5[b]	~66.5
1955	5,640	2,820	~25	11,280	~7.5[b]	~67.5
1960	6,174	3,087	~22	12,348	~10.5[c]	~67.5
1965	7,154	3,577	~21	14,308	~12[d]	~67

SOURCES: (a) Data in these columns taken from table 33. (b) U.S. Bureau of the Census, *Historical Statistics of the United States: Colonial Times to 1957* (Washington, D.C., 1960), p. 163, series G2-14. (c) U.S. Bureau of the Census, *Historical Statistics of the United States: Continuation to 1962* (Washington, D.C., 1965), p. 22. (d) Estimated.

earlier levels. This last finding of a resurgence in the ranks of the affluent stands in noteworthy conflict with the egalitarian tendencies inherent in the remaining figures in table 36.

SEVEN

Social Responsibility for Welfare

IN WHAT RESPECTS and to what extent is *society*, working through the instrumentality of the state, responsible for the welfare of its members? What demands for the promotion of his welfare can an individual reasonably make upon his society? These are questions to which no answer can be given in terms of some a priori approach with reference to universal ultimates. Whatever answer can appropriately be given will depend, in the final analysis, *on what the society decides it should be.* The questions carry us back straightaway to first principles of government. On any democratic conception of the issue, the propriety of governmental activity must be determined in accordance with "the consent of the governed" and must thus result from an explicit decision of the body politic. The purposes whose realization is pursued by any truly democratic government must ultimately be derived from a nation's public mandate.

The use of *decides* in the formula given above is a somewhat exaggerated anthropomorphism, as when one speaks of a "social contract." What is basically at issue is a complex mixture of accreted custom and positive law, defining the range of legitimate demands and so creating the basis for warranted expectations and claims. In a specifically democratic society, the state *has* responsibility for welfare in all regards in which the processes of democratic government have *endowed* it therewith.

One recent writer on social philosophy has maintained that "the very fact that welfare is so generally desired makes it reasonable to demand that governments should guarantee it, and if necessary provide the material basis [of welfare] themselves."[1] However, the basic reason why people are justified in looking to the state for support of their welfare, and why this expectation is something other than highly unreasonable, is surely not that welfare is desirable and generally desired. A great many things are desirable and generally desired![2] Rather, such justification is to be sought in the fact that the state *has been duly charged* by the public mandate with the proper execution of this task, as determined by the political process.

Conservative thinkers (traditional liberals of the Millian stamp not excluded) have resisted governmental action in the economic area on the grounds that such an expansion of state functions rests upon a misapprehension or even distortion of the proper work of the state, as heretofore conceived. Such opposition usually tended to be based on some version of the very mistaken notion that there is such a thing as a timelessly fixed concept of the proper work of the state per se. But in fact the state is an instrumentality of its people; it gets its mandate from them, and if they *want* it to serve a certain function, and assign this function to it through the political process, then that is that—this function has thereby become part of "the proper work" of the state. The question, of course, remains as to what people *ought* to want the state to do, including whether the state is in a position in terms of its resources and capabilities effectively and efficiently to shoulder this assigned task or whether it would not be better to work for the realization of this aim by other means. But this does not affect the basic fact that the state obtains its missions and responsibilities from an a posteriori mandate of its members, not a priori from some edict writ large in the nature of things.

The standard political issue of *legitimation* arises also with regard to the welfare obligations of the state. The state is responsible for the discharge of a mission only when and as duly charged with

---

1. Brian Barry, *Political Argument* (London, 1968), p. 188.
2. Religious services and sex are only some examples of things "generally desired" that Americans, at any rate, would be reluctant to permit the government to oversee.

it through the appropriate workings of the machinery of public decision. (And here, as usual, the question of legitimacy must be distinguished from that of effectiveness. With welfare as with national defense, national processes may be inefficient or national resources inadequate to demands. Indeed, in a state responsive to the will of an insatiable and unrealistic electorate, measures nominally taken in support of the general welfare may result in grossly compromising it.)

In line with these considerations, the move from a family of *social indicators* as such to yardsticks for measuring how well the state is "meeting its welfare responsibilities" hinges on the settlement of a prior political question, namely, what the welfare commitments of the state are to be. The answer to this question is not deducible from the nature of things but results from the processes of social decision. The electorate's expectation of governmental concern for welfare is warranted by the fact that it has commissioned the state to be concerned. In this regard the present public view is a revolutionary reversal of that of nineteenth-century America with its stress upon the pioneering spirit, personal self-sufficiency, and independence. Compulsory education, social-security legislation, public-health regulations, and all the mechanisms of the welfare state we nowadays accept unhesitatingly as legitimate areas of governmental concern are utterly antithetical to the then-current views of the responsibility of the individual and the proper mission of government.

The conception of a person's dependency on others has changed drastically in modern times in such a way as to bring the society as a whole more and more prominently upon the stage. I cannot better describe this phenomenon than by quotation from an important essay written by Richard M. Titmuss, "The Social Division of Welfare":

With the gradual break-up of the old poor law, more "states of dependency" have been defined and recognized as collective responsibilities, and more differential provision has been made in respect to them. These "states of dependency" arise for the vast majority of the population whenever they are not in a position to "earn life" for themselves and their families; they are then dependent people. In industrialized societies there are many causes of dependency; they may be "natural dependencies" as in childhood, extreme old age and child-bearing. They may be causes by physical and psychological ill-health and incapacity; in part, these are culturally determined dependencies. Or they may be wholly or predominently determined by social and cultural factors. These, it may be said, are the "man-made" dependencies. Apart from injury, disease and innate incapacity, they now constitute the major source of instability in the satisfaction of basic needs. They include unemployment and under-employment, protective and preventive legislation, compulsory retirement from work, the delayed entry of young people into the labour market, and an infinite variety of subtle cultural factors ranging from the "right" trade union ticket to the possession of an assortment of status symbols. All may involve to some degree the destruction, curtailment, interruption or frustration of earning power in the individual, and more pronounced secondary dependencies when they further involve the wives, children, and other relatives. In general, many of these culturally determined dependencies have grown in range and significance over the past century, partly as a result of a process of cumulative survivorship, for those who experience such states of dependency do not now die as others did before the twentieth century.[3]

Thus in the context of social welfare the root conception of dependency of an incapacitated person upon his natural guardians has undergone a massive and far-reaching transformation in regard to matters of public policy. The causative factors operative here lie primarily in the region of scale and complexity. The ideal of the good Samaritan who relies wholly upon his own resources to remedy a wrong is no longer an effective paradigm in the context of the social maladies inherent in the mass phenomenon of contemporary life.[4]

This step of charging the state with responsibility for the welfare of its people is certainly not just a matter of arbitrary fiat. With the enormous expansion of the welfare state over the past generation, a questioning of the *justification* of the enormous accretion of state functions in the welfare area is certainly perfectly legitimate. There are, of course, reasonable limits to the extent of state responsibility for the public welfare. These can be set with

3. *Essays on "the Welfare State"* (New Haven, Conn., 1959), pp. 42-43.
4. For a development of this theme, see Thomas F. Green, *Work, Leisure, and the American Schools* (New York, 1968), pp. 115-46.

reference to certain criteria that spell out the lines of criticism of state activity in this sphere. Some examples follow:

1. *Realism and effectiveness.* A society whose economy is realtively poor cannot afford welfare-supportive programs comparable to those of a society whose economy is relatively prosperous. And clearly there are limits to the extent to which *any* society, even an affluent one, can afford to commit resources to the furtherance of welfare.[5] Correspondingly, to hold the state responsible for doing more in the welfare area than it can actually manage, and to require it to go outside the area where it can operate effectively, is to transgress the bounds of realism and to lay a groundwork for frustration and bitterness of disappointed expectations.

2. *Efficiency.* The mechanisms of state action are almost al-

5. In earlier days the conception was widespread that a beneficent deity kept zealous watch upon the welfare of mankind. Philosopher upon philosopher played variations upon this theme, but I shall content myself with one passage from Descartes.

Experience makes us aware that all the feelings with which nature inspires us are such as I have just spoken of; and there is therefore nothing in them which does not give testimony to the power and goodness of the God who has produced them. Thus, for example, when the nerves which are in the feet are violently or more than usually moved, their movement, passing through the medulla of the spine to the inmost parts of the brain, gives a sign to the mind which makes it feel somewhat, to wit, pain, as though in the foot, by which the mind is excited to do its utmost to remove the cause of the evil as dangerous and hurtful to the foot. It is true that God could have constituted the nature of man in such a way that this same movement in the brain would have conveyed something quite different to the mind; for example, it might have produced consciousness of itself either in so far as it is in the brain, or as it is in the foot, or as it is in some other place between the foot and the brain, or it might finally have produced consciousness of anything else whatsoever; but none of all this would have contributed so well to the conservation of the body. Similarly, when we desire to drink, a certain dryness of the throat is produced which moves its nerves, and by their means and internal portions of the brain; and this movement causes in the mind the sensation of thirst, because in this case there is nothing more useful to us than to become aware that we have need to drink for the conservation of our health; and the same holds good in other instances. (*Meditations on First Philosophy*, no. VI, in *Collected Works of Descartes*, trans. E. S. Haldane and G. R. T. Ross [Cambridge, 1911-1912])

Such confidence in God's concern for human welfare is manifest throughout Descartes's system. More recently, of course, secularization has set in with respect to God's solicitude for man's welfare (as with so much else) with the state now put into God's place. But one must never forget that Leviathan is unlike Jehovah in one crucial respect: he is not omnipotent.

ways cumbersome, especially when bureaucratic institutionalization becomes involved. (Think of Parkinson's Law.) Many kinds of welfare-promoting activities are presumably best left to smaller and more diversified agencies other than that of the state, agencies that can work more effectively because they are closer to "the grass roots" (private individuals, families, nongovernmental institutions, and the like).[6]

3. *Protection of rights.* The desideratum of maintaining an open society and avoiding totalitarianism will limit the sphere of state action on behalf of social welfare, lest the welfare-supportive action contravene the legitimate rights of individuals.[7] Some examples of these limits would be the restriction of "preventive detention," the curtailment of wiretapping as an investigative method, and the prohibition of group punishment for individual malfunction. The protection of rights is a particular, but particularly important, special case of the general principle to which we now turn.

4. *Conflicts of objectives.* The drawing of limits to a society's welfare commitments may be justified in terms of its protection of *other* values. In prizing individual initiative, for example, the society may well limit its activities on behalf of welfare because it espouses a conception of "the good life" for man that delimits the range of what others should do to promote a person's welfare and correspondingly defines the extent to which he should "fend for himself."

Points 3 and 4 of this list express a line of thought which, while perhaps not altogether popular at present, certainly lies at the

6. To say this of some welfare measures is, of course, not to deny that others can best be administered at the national level, either because greater efficiency and economy can be had by operating on a larger scale or because this is necessary to attain across-the-board uniformity. But the point is that in many cases flexibility, innovation, and an adjustment to local needs and conditions are important, but very difficult to attain under the state's aegis.

7. The classic and, to modern ears, greatly exaggerated statement of this position is Herbert Spencer's *Social Statics* (London, 1851; American ed., New York, 1892). Spencer categorically opposed any departure from laissez faire to protect individuals against consequences of their own foolishness: "The invalid is at liberty to buy medicine and advice from whomsoever he pleases; the unlicensed practitioner is at liberty to sell to whosoever will buy. On no pretext can a barrier be set up between the two without the law of equal freedom being broken" (p. 201).

core of traditional liberal democratic theory. Alexis de Tocqueville
was already apprehensive lest the state become for its citizens

an immense and tutelary power, which takes upon itself alone to secure
their gratifications, and to watch over their fate. . . . For their happiness
such a government willingly labours, but it chooses to be the sole agent
and the only arbiter of that happiness: it provides for their security,
foresees and supplies their necessities, facilitates their pleasures, man-
ages their principal concerns, directs their industry, regulates the de-
scent of property, and subdivides their inheritances—what remains, but
to spare them all the care of thinking and all the trouble of living? . . .
The will of man is not shattered, but softened, bent, and guided: men
are seldom forced to act, but they are constantly restrained from acting:
such a power does not destroy, but it prevents existence; it does not
tyrannize, but it compresses, enervates, extinguishes, and stupefies a
people, till each nation is reduced to be nothing better than a flock of
timid and industrious animals, of which the government is the shep-
herd.[8]

That classic study of democratic liberalism, J. S. Mill's essay, *On
Liberty*, is also eloquently prophetic about the slippery slope that
leads the state from social benevolence to a baneful paternalism
that undermines all individual initiative and personal responsibility. The case built up in this way is doubtless not decisive, but it is
certainly sufficient in the first analysis. With welfare, as in other
contexts, the presumption goes against action by the state: other
things being anything like equal, individuals can be left to act for
themselves. Only in cases of incapacity or disability, and in circumstances that can legitimately be assimilated to these, can the
warrant for state intervention outweigh the threat of potentially
negative consequences inherent in the resolution of problems
through the instrumentality of state action.

To consider in clear perspective the complex issue of the state's
involvements with the welfare of its members, one must distinguish two aspects of the public welfare of persons coexisting in a
social environment: the distributive and the collective. *Distributive welfare* has to do with personal resources at the disposal of the
individual within the scope of his own means. *Collective welfare*

8. A. de Tocqueville, *Democracy in America*, ed. H. S. Commager (New York,
1946), pp. 579-80.

has to do with public resources that provide for various aspects of the welfare of people in general through the maintenance of systematic societal instrumentalities. The possession of an automobile relates to a person's distributive welfare; the road system on which he operates it and the network of filling stations that serve to keep it in operation relate to the collective sector.

The American economy has reached a level of productivity that underwrites a widespread affluence throughout our society. A point has been reached where people can, or with an added modicum of egalitarian redistribution could, perfectly well be put into a position of providing for their personal welfare needs. An economy that is adequately productive and adequately egalitarian could dismantle, or at any rate transform, a part of the machinery of the welfare state. In this event, the state could in large measure take itself out of the *distributive*-welfare business, outside the traditional range of special categories (orphans, the aged, the incapacitated, etc.). Instead, the state could concentrate on the *collective*-welfare functions regarding the publicly shared conditions of our common environment. For increasing affluence does not automatically solve all welfare problems, since these do not lie solely in the area of the goods and services an individual can command but extend to that of the common environment he shares systematically with his fellows.

This point of view has an intimate connection with the central thesis of John Kenneth Galbraith's classic study, *The Affluent Society*.[9] Basic to his approach is the distinction between the private sector of individual consumption and the public sector of the goods and services for common ends (public works, public housing, law enforcement, urban renewal and beautification, public parks, and so on). Galbraith argues that there is a serious imbalance in the division of the resources of our society between these two sectors, with far too much going to private consumption and far too little to the public sector that substantially determines our common physical and man-made environment, producing the glaring disparity of private affluence amid public squalor. This leads Galbraith to

9. John Kenneth Galbraith, *The Affluent Society* (Boston, 1958).

urge a revision in public policy, with collective action to make up for the neglected sector of public goods.[10]

This desirable and indeed necessary shift encounters serious impedance from the individualistic orientation traditional to the American value system, with its strongly negative orientation toward the commitment of public resources for the realization of social objectives apart from the traditional ones of national defense and maintaining the economy. Yet, as we have seen, there are definite signs that this aspect of our value orientation is changing. Under the pressure of the needs and opportunities of a highly technological, industrialized, affluent yet diversified society, Americans are moving increasingly toward a more collective value orientation. Certainly, our common environment—natural and artificial—has become an unavoidable addition to the sectors of legitimate large-scale investment of public resources, a phenomenon that brings in its train a significant enhancement of socially oriented values.[11] This shift in values is readily accounted for along the lines of the cost-benefit model of value change detailed above. In this regard, it is not affluence as such, but the conditions under which it is realized in current circumstances—technological advancement and economic sophistication, social complexity and urban crowding—that are the operative factors in establishing the urgency of other-regarding considerations. The social and economic conditions that present themselves at the current juncture of American history are such that an adherence to the social point of view—as regards both the distributive sector of welfare and its collective sector—is of common benefit to everyone in furthering his personal welfare. The way in which we ourselves act as individuals affects the makeup of our common physical and social en-

10. This obviously poses the question of whether *collective* action is necessarily to be glossed as *governmental* action. May not other channels of activity be better suited to the task, and, specifically, could needs of the public sector of consumption not be met from the private sector of production? We shall return to this issue later. At this point, let it suffice to cite David Braybrooke's suggestive article "Private Production of Public Goods," in *Values and the Future*, eds. K. Baier and N. Rescher (New York, 1969), pp. 368-88.

11. This view and its evidence are developed in greater detail in the writer's contributions to Baier and Rescher, *Values and the Future*.

vironment—the systematic context in which we must all alike operate—in such a way that if we cause its degradation for some, the network of interconnections is strong enough to assure its degradation for ourselves as well. And the price of failure in terms of social disorder and environmental degradation is one that would exact substantial penalties for each and every American.

Serious and complex issues lurk in the relationship of the general welfare to human rights. An interesting case in point occurs when a man has a double dose of the Y sex chromosome, making him a prime candidate for the "double Y syndrome" in that men in this condition apparently have an inherent genetic tendency toward antisocial, aggressive behavior. Would control measures over such persons taken in the name of the general welfare be justified? Suppose it was established that middle-aged males were extraordinarily accident-prone as automobile drivers during hours of darkness at the time of a full moon. Legislation closing the roads to them at these times would (*ex hypothesi*) contribute significantly toward the general welfare. But would it not also contravene a reasonable construction of their "rights"? Or take a more drastic case. What if only (as actually seems to be the case in substantial measure) the children of the urban ghetto in America could be lifted out of the culture of poverty by being shifted from this environment into a kibbutz-like situation? One might well, however, want to see the rights of individuals safeguarded in certain cases even despite the general welfare.[12] (This, of course, cuts both ways. One can, legitimately, expect people to yield certain of their rights and privileges to *some* extent in the furtherance of the general welfare.)

The difficulties arising from a potential conflict between welfare and rights are frequently overlooked by writers on social issues. Thus in one recent source we read: "Besides invoking the concept of personal rights to evaluate governments, advocates of democracy make use of the concept of human welfare. They could

---

12.   One recent writer quite rightly observes that one might well "want to reserve for certain rights—the right to a fair trial; or the right to equal treatment before the law—a place outside the scope of . . . debate [about welfare]" (David Braybrooke, *Three Tests for Democracy: Personal Rights, Human Welfare, Collective Preference* [New York, 1968]).

perhaps dispense with the concept of rights, if they accept rights simply as means of advancing welfare."[13] But such a subsumption of rights under *welfare* would require bloating this concept out of all recognition, in order to comprehend somehow "the good of man" in all of its endlessly diversified forms. Such concept imperialism serves no useful purpose. The move in the reverse direction, an endeavor to subsume welfare under rights, is more plausible. (Think here of the currently popular cliché of "welfare rights.") But this step would lead toward the very conclusions being argued here: that since there is a plurality of legitimate rights, the claims of each are bounded and conditioned by the others, and that the protection of rights in a community (i.e., nonwelfare rights) can, on occasion, call for steps that are counterproductive from the limited aspect of the general welfare alone.[14]

When other persons are responsible for someone's welfare, what can they be expected to do about it—just how far does their responsibility extend? Clearly, this will have to vary with the specific nature of the relationship at issue and, in the special case of a society as a whole, will hinge largely on where the society itself chooses to set the limits. But it would certainly be inappropriate to stretch those limits beyond a certain point. It is not reasonable to view society as standing *in loco parentis* to its members, with the virtually open-ended responsibilities predominately held operative in this regard throughout the West. In this far-reaching parental regard, society should at most take on the role of *a parent of last resort*, providing for the welfare of those whose circumstances pose excessive or impracticable burdens upon their own resources and those of their natural guardians: relationless orphans, the handicapped, the insane, etc.

But, of course, most of the welfare responsibilities of society lie

13. Ibid., p. 86. My critique of this particular passage should not cloud appreciation of the great value and fundamental right-mindedness of the analysis of the relation of rights and welfare in this work.

14. Braybrooke rightly points out that "Marxist writers concern themselves with human welfare, but avoid endorsing rights for fear of compromising themselves with bourgeois ideology" (ibid., p. 88). Moreover, a recognition of people's rights can often raise havoc with the administrative efficiency of a centralized apparatus of control.

outside this parental sector and relate to society's commitments
not to the predominantly helpless, but to the vastly greater rest.
It is, in this connection, useful and conducive to clarity to differen-
tiate between first-line and second-line responsibility for welfare.
In exercising first-line responsibility, a person himself undertakes
to provide for the welfare of a subject; the person with second-line
responsibility merely helps his subject to provide for his own welfare. (The latter can take many forms: the creation of opportunities, the provision of facilities, the encouragement of initiative, the
material support requisite for the subject's action on his own behalf, and so on.) The parent of small children, of course, has first-
line responsibility for the welfare of his offspring; and a society
may, as we have maintained, reasonably be held to stand fully *in
loco parentis* in certain extraordinary cases—with respect to special categories of its members such as those who are drastically
handicapped, physically or mentally. But by and large, apart from
such special circumstances, it is unreasonable to charge society
with more than second-line responsibility for the welfare of its
members. In the support of personal welfare, the individual himself and his family are posted in the front line, bearing a responsibility that the instrumentalities of society should, insofar as possible, support but not supplant. To step beyond these limits is to
invite socially harmful consequences: the erosion of personal initiative, the undermining of people's self-image, the fostering of attitudes of dependency, the weakening of the bonds of meaningful
human relationships, and the like.

We have maintained that by and large, throughout most of the
range of ordinary cases, the person himself is responsible for provision for his own welfare. But what if he is not unable but simply
reluctant in this regard: what can the other people of his social environment reasonably be expected to do then? The question arises:
Under what circumstances are others justified in intervening when
a person neglects his own welfare? Obviously such interference is
legitimate in parental circumstances and in those other special
categories where, from the very nature of the case, it would be
unreasonable to hold the subjects themselves responsible because
they are simply incapable (for some valid reason or other) of act-

ing effectively on their own behalf. But what of other cases where the blockage is not so much a matter of inability as unwillingness?

The appropriate solution to this problem seems to reside in the principle that persons are entitled to interfere in regard to someone else's welfare when his welfare is systematically interconnected with theirs in such a way that his neglect of his welfare endangers their own interests (their welfare, their rights, etc.). The prime examples are provided by the collective-welfare issues: air pollution, vehicular-traffic regulation, urban-noise restrictions, the regulation of communicable diseases, etc. In such cases, the man who acts with indifference to his own welfare also compromises that of others. The man who neglects his health on a crowded ship or who lets his house become a fire hazard in a densely populated town does not endanger himself alone. In such circumstances, others who are involved certainly have valid grounds of justification for intervention, grounds whose strength will, of course, vary with the nature of the case. (Endangering the life or health of another is one thing; setting him an example of poor manners is another.)

The collective-welfare issues gain special import and prominence under the conditions of urban crowding and mass interaction in modern industrialized societies. In a way, we are all living on a crowded ship nowadays, "the spaceship earth." The condition of our common environment—physical, economic, social, biomedical—defines a collective sector of welfare that contains many matters of legitimate public responsibility: air and water pollution control, public health, crime control, and so on. Moreover, it is not only the prevention of the harmful and negative that is at issue, but also the promotion of those beneficial and positive aspects of our natural and man-made environment, such as the provision of public services in the areas of television, transport, postal and electronic communication, etc. This whole area of our common environment has to do with the systematic, person-transcending sector of welfare, where the welfare interests of people in general blend into one vast interconnected network. In this sphere, people cannot (in principle) act as individuals in the furtherance of certain aspects of their welfare. They must, in the very nature of things, act in concert with others in such a way that coordination—even forcible coordination—may be necessary.

It is crucial that this discussion concerns *welfare* and not *happiness* itself. People's welfare is interlinked by invisible threads; the man who endangers his own can in many ways endanger that of others. The direct responsibility for at least some major aspects of an individual's welfare can thus justifiably be seen as not lying solely in the hands of the individual himself, but also resting with the society in general. But this is certainly not true as regards happiness. In point of happiness, it is the individual himself who, for better or worse, must bear the entire direct responsibility for his own fate.[15] A world in which the responsibility for individual happiness lies with the state directly—and not merely indirectly, in the creation of incentives, the opening up of opportunities, the facilitation of individual efforts, and the like—would be a world that is not a utopia but a horror. To accept this horror for the alleged sake of "the greater happiness of the greater number" is to espouse the convenient but ultimately poisonous policy of exalting ends above means.

The present discussion has to this juncture dealt primarily with the claims that the individual can make upon his society. But the reverse issue must also be examined. What sacrifice of his own welfare in the interest of that of the general group can a society or state reasonably expect of, and indeed exact from, a member individual?

Obviously the extent of justifiably exactable sacrifice will depend altogether upon the circumstances. Historically, the conception has been that when the very survival of the society is at stake (as in certain cases of war and insurrection), a virtually total sacrifice can legitimately be demanded. No doubt, in the present century, adhesion to this concept has declined in the wake of the disillusionment produced by two major and countless minor wars. All the same, an impressive case can yet be made to support the traditional conception that a society (at any rate a free, open, demo-

---

15. To say this is not, of course, to deny that society can act *in loco parentis* with respect to a minor or to safeguard, not only his health but, his ultimate chances in "the pursuit of happiness."

cratic society) is warranted in demanding substantial sacrifices from its members in those circumstances when its survival as the sort of society it is are genuinely at stake.

But obviously—and fortunately—the cases at issue in the context of welfare are generally not of this extreme survival-determining kind; they deal mainly with the lesser but yet painful sacrifices of money, "status," personal convenience, and the like. A perhaps typical example is something like the construction of a crosstown expressway or an airport, involving the dislocation of some and the infliction of a nuisance upon many. The rational establishment of a warrant for such a measure is a very complex issue, but the following three factors will in any case be prominent here:

1. *Cost-benefit justification.* It must be shown (1) that the negative consequences for some are in the broadest perspective significantly outweighed by the positive benefits for others and (2) that the measure at issue is such that there is no alternative that would yield all or most of these benefits at lesser social costs.

2. *Political equity.* The social group can justifiably exact from each member only those sacrifices that would also be expected of all others in like circumstances. And any sacrifices to be made "in the common interest" must reflect a genuine community of interest in which those who bear the onus themselves have a significant stake. Moreover, their sacrifice must be determined upon in conformity with the standard canons of social justice (equity, due process, etc.).

3. *Compensation.* Insofar as the circumstances of the case allow, reasonable provision must be made for shielding those who can be shielded and for compensating those who must bear unavoidably the negative consequences of generally beneficial measures.

The upshot of this line of thought is this: society can indeed expect individuals to sacrifice their welfare for the common good, but it is *justified* in doing so only in those circumstances where a combination of demonstrable public benefit and maintenance of proper safeguards of individual rights and interests conspires to constitute a proper warrant for this step.

The individual may thus legitimately be asked to sink his personal-welfare interests in certain delimited respects into the general good. In the course, for example, of protecting society against the hardened criminal and the dangerously insane, a society may well (and defensibly) find it necessary on occasion to compromise the welfare of some in the interests of the general welfare as a whole (e.g., through an "invasion of privacy"). In such cases, individual welfare may defensibly be subordinated to a degree to the general welfare of the group. And this is not all. One critical consideration should never be allowed to drop from sight: a state has obligations other than the welfare of its citizens. Certain of these arise in its dealings with other states (honoring its commitments, maintaining its integrity and self-respect, etc.). Others regard the management of its internal affairs (safeguarding individual rights, maintaining due process of law, keeping aloft its values and ideals, etc.). The coordinated realization of this multitude of responsibilities means that on occasion some may be subordinated to others. A society's responsibilities for welfare are not limited by its means alone, but by its other responsibilities as well.[16]

16. For a classical discussion of many facets of the problems discussed in the present chapter, see John Stuart Mill's great essay *On Liberty* (London, 1859). For an interesting contemporary treatment of a whole host of relevant issues, see Barry, *Political Argument.*

EIGHT

The Political Dimension of Welfare

1. Welfare and Planning

IT IS A MATTER of immense difficulty to assure that people's welfare is adequately provided for under the complex conditions of the crowded, pluralistic, inegalitarian yet generally affluent, technologically advanced, modern mass society of contemporary America. This is particularly true in a time of rapid social and economic change.[1] Of the forces operative here, none rivals the revolutionary impact of modern industrial technology. This new technology has forged a wholly different economic environment in which many old skills are no longer in demand and entire new professions are springing up. To realize generally agreed-upon social-welfare objectives under such conditions requires the meshed cooperative effort of the institutions of society at many levels. The random and uncoordinated goodwill of individuals acting in the traditional channels of "charity" has proved entirely insufficient to the magnitude of the problem and has given way to "public assistance." The requirements of the situation have led, pretty much inescapably, to the centralism of state, to action through public institutions at various levels. And this centralism, together with an urge toward efficiency and effectiveness, establishes a need for planning. Cen-

---

1. One provocative recent study indicates that technological growth has been generally exponential in the present century, doubling every twenty years in nations having advanced technology. See A. L. Shef, "Socio-Economic Attributes of Our Technological Society" (Study presented to the IEEE [Institute of Electrical and Electronic Engineers] Wescon Conference, Los Angeles, August 1968).

tralized effort and synoptic planning have thus been pervasive features of social-welfare provision throughout the present century, imposed upon us despite individualist inclinations by the forces already indicated: the *scale* of activity, the *scope* of the needed resources, and the *rapidity* of social and technological change.[2]

Another factor that reinforces the role of planning in relation to welfare is the inevitable future-orientedness of many welfare measures, which operate in a context where it is imperative to look ahead. As a person must brush his teeth in the present to guard against dental problems in the future, so a society must take preventive action now against potential future welfare problems through provisions for public health, schooling, job-retraining, etc. Society must act in innumerable ways today to safeguard welfare for tomorrow. And the deployment of rational foresight to guide present action in the light of potential future contingencies is, of course, the very essence of planning.

Welfare planning, moreover, is necessary from yet another point of view. Many measures for the general welfare involve an inescapably unequal distribution of burdens and advantages in the interests of realizing the general good. The building of roads, the construction of dams, the placement of power stations, the location of airfields and the fixing of air-traffic routings, the placement of schools, and the like, all involve the imposition of a substantial nuisance upon many people. Without careful planning, the cost-benefit equation that results in all such cases cannot be solved in the most favorable way, as it is obvious in "the general interest" that it should be. A society's effective pursuit of the welfare of its members calls for a high degree of administrative rationality and so establishes yet another requirement for planning.

When public-welfare measures move from the status of plans to operational reality, they entail public expenditures. To judge by recent experience throughout the West, the costs of welfare measures are not only real but very large, and there is every reason to

2. For one recent discussion that brings home the need for planning under contemporary circumstances in a forceful way, see Geoffrey Vicker's stimulating essay "The End of Free Fall" in his *Value Systems and Social Process* (New York, 1968), pp. 52-70.

expect them to continue their climb upward in the foreseeable future. Provision for welfare calls for the allocation of enormous resources, committing a massive quantity of socially available assets to meeting socially recognized needs. When the society, through its instrument of collective action, the state, assumes certain tasks of collective-welfare provision, it undertakes to allocate public resources (i.e., resources which are, or can be made, available by the public) to the realization of benefits for its individual members. But, of course, a society cannot synthesize assets *ex nihilo*; it can only redeploy existing assets for the realization of welfare aims. When the society assumes a part of the welfare mission, it must be willing *and able* to pay the price. This factor of affordability is critical. A poor society cannot afford to carry the welfare burden of a rich one. And even a wealthy society may be unable or unwilling to pay the price for realizing "generally desired" ends. For example, the widely lamented pollution of America's water resources, which has been at the forefront of public consciousness since the appearance of Rachel Carson's celebrated *Silent Spring*,[3] could be completely avoided by the utilization of presently available engineering systems. But, lamentably, the public's interest in making the needed economic (and political) readjustments is grossly insufficient. Here the problem is basically one of economic resources, but more drastic cases also arise. The limitation of population size is generally conceded as a desirable social objective, but any of the (perfectly feasible) measures of explicit social control (e.g., "parenthood by license only") is obviously unacceptable under current conditions on political grounds.

The budgetary aspect of the matter brings into focus another aspect of welfare planning, namely, the question of *alternative* allocation of resources. It is clear that the "public-welfare sector" is only one alternative among many demands competing for the expenditure of funds available to the society. Some major areas of public expenditure with which welfare measures must compete in the distribution of resources are national security, culture and education (at any rate that nonbasic and nonvocational education which itself does not come within the sphere of welfare provi-

3. Rachel Carson, *Silent Spring* (Boston, 1962).

sions), the "private sector" of individual consumption, and future-oriented social and economic investments in the public sector. (Welfare, as we have repeatedly stressed, is not, and should not be, a be-all and end-all.) All such competing pressures circumscribe and restrict the volume of social investment in the support of welfare. This fact points to another critical aspect of welfare planning: in view of the operative limitations, it is essential that the greatest possible effectiveness should be realized in public-welfare outlays. For to expend inefficiently or ineffectually the limited funds available is to fail tragically the essential interests and urgent needs of the consumers of public welfare.

Society need not, of course, act as an aggregate unit; it can also act in a decentralized way through a market economy to provide individuals with what they need and want. There can be little doubt that the best public-welfare measure is a *healthy economy* that creates sufficient goods and services to fill needs all around. By providing sufficiently many and sufficiently good jobs, an affluent economy lets people earn enough to attend to their own welfare needs, at any rate in the sector of distributive needs (perhaps leaving only collective-welfare needs to be provided by public action). It cannot be overemphasized that a healthy economy is perhaps the best welfare measure.

In stressing the economic aspect of welfare planning, we must not lose sight of its sociopsychological side. A social-welfare measure that achieves economically desirable results at the cost of socially undesirable consequences may be a tragic failure. Some recent urban-renewal projects in various American cities graphically illustrate this point. Despite the economic successes of these projects in removing slums, creating jobs, and the like, they have, on balance, proved dismal failures because they have destroyed *neighborhoods*—life-environments for weaving positively valued patterns of individual and communal interaction. The people dislocated may have gained in terms of a newer and better habitation, but at a price of social dislocation and disruption they would themselves far rather not have paid.

To say that welfare planning is necessary is not to say that it is easy. Indeed, its problems and difficulties are massively formidable. One prime difficulty is that of assuring that the actual effects of a measure in fact conform to its intended objectives. It is a distressingly common phenomenon to find a wide gulf between the glowing rhetoric advanced at the hopeful initiation of a welfare measure and the modest, nay, often squalid, reality that it actually achieves. Throughout the social-welfare area, hopefully constructive measures are fraught with unintended and unforeseen side effects and unenvisaged complications. A striking example of this is given by the "Moynihan thesis" that public-welfare measures intended to assist indigent mothers of small children (by granting them an allowance when there is no husband in the household capable of contributing earnings to it) have encouraged a breakdown of the family structure among impoverished American Negroes by making it economically disadvantageous for mothers of illegitimate children to transform a random liaison into permanent cohabitation. Intended only to help mothers and children, the welfare measures at issue have worked substantial harm to all the parties concerned, discouraging the creation of family units and so blocking the development of mature adult relationships, diminishing responsible care for children, discouraging parental initiative and responsibility, etc. This example illustrates the way in which, given the complex interweaving of social forces, measures intended to work for the general good can issue general harm. Intelligent planning for the social welfare cannot but be a matter of extreme difficulty, if we are to avoid such untoward side effects. This type of planning is best done by careful and cautious step-by-step pragmatic experimentation rather than bold measures derived from large-scale social doctrines and based on elaborate theories. (But to insist on intelligent planning and to hold that this at its best is cautious and gradualistic, effecting hoped-for improvements by evolutionary rather than revolutionary steps, are not, of course, to deny the need for planning as such.)

The prime social objective in the sphere of public welfare is the creation of a set of arrangements in all relevant areas—economic, biomedical, and educational—to assure that the welfare interests of all people are duly secured. The critical task here is that of forging a social and economic order to achieve these basic objectives, be it by the unfettered workings of a free market or through some degree of regulation. The reader must not be mislead in this connection by the emphasis that has been placed upon planning. For there is a wide difference between centralized public *planning* for realization of the social welfare on the one hand and, on the other, centralized public *control* for the realization of these objectives.

The implementation of planning does indeed require coordination and mutual adjustment, but this need not call for any comprehensive centralized control in the sense of actual direction, let alone dictation. It may well—nay, usually does—turn out to be quite sufficient to operate in this area with a partial control and a large measure of incentives (both positive and negative). The health aspects of welfare afford a good example of this: only a very modest list of health measures are legally mandatory, and the incentives of individual concern are allowed free play over a very wide area. And much the same picture can prevail on the economic side of public welfare in the American situation, with a modicum of control to assure, for example, national uniformity in the provision of certain minimal essentials but a wide scope for incentives to encourage innovation and creativity.

This line of thought points to the conception of what might be called *second-order centralism*: a system of planning and its implementation without actual operational control of the activities at issue and consequently with first-order decentralization. The regulation of vehicular traffic in cities affords a good example of the workings of this conception. No driver is constrained to use a certain route. But some are made easier than others (by supplementing the natural differences with such artificial instrumentalities as traffic lights, stop signs, and the like), with the result that the traffic in a given direction can be channeled in a predictable way along selected routings in a manner which, as far as concerns the motorist himself, is entirely free of the factor of control. Often, control in the domain of social and economic arrangements is simply indicative of a failure of "social engineering": a failure of society to realize desired objectives by less drastic means. Sometimes, of course, actual control is unavoidable. (On the traffic analogy, think now not of automobiles but of aircraft near heavily used airways and airfields.) The optimal arrangement is doubtless a mixture into which control enters at some points, producing a balance of directive elements with elements of incentive. The key fact is that the requirement for the implementation of plans as such need not result in any pervasive *control* over the activities planned for. Planning without operational control is more than a possibility, it is an ongoing reality in many spheres of human life. One influential professional view puts the matter in a way that cannot be improved upon:

Moreover, in the broad sense of the term, "planning" involves more than the allocation of national resources. It involves efforts to identify needs, crystallize goals, appraise resources and outline coordinated steps to meet these goals at every level of social or political organization—using all the mechanisms appropriate and acceptable under prevailing law and custom. In a pluralistic society like our own, these include not only a wide range and level of governmental mechanisms but an even wider range of nongovernmental devices operating under the dynamics of the profit motive or voluntary association for mutual ends. Inevitably these interact with governmental bodies to play a "planning" role in the developmental process. In fact, one measure of development may well be the variety, complexity, stability, and effectiveness of the many organizational devices needed to make a modern industrial society function and advance toward the achievement of welfare goals.[4]

Any realistic view of the requisites of rational planning for welfare must distinguish the *centralism* of coordination to assure a reasonable result from the *concentration* of power to produce this result by explicit direction. Welfare-supportive measures are not always best decided upon by bureaucratic administrators in a remote decision-making center such as Washington or Whitehall. The planner may be well positioned to determine ends and set standards but is often in a poor position to determine the specific manner, means, and timing for their implementation. Here extensive knowledge of the details of particular cases is often called for —knowledge often more readily available to the man on the spot than to some remote bureaucrat. Failure to heed this limitation

4. Elizabeth Wickenden, *Social Welfare in a Changing World* (Washington, D.C., 1965), p. 9.

carries substantial dangers in its wake. Throughout the twentieth century the conception of "the managed society" of the "social engineers" has been coming into increasing prominence. The passage of years has brought an ever more powerful central government concerned to assume the "welfare" of its people in an ever more expanding sense. Projecting recent trends far enough—and, to be sure, this is always a risky thing to do—one arrives at the frightening vision of the state as an all-powerful authority which regulates in great detail virtually every facet of the public and private lives of its people "in their own interest." As we see it, this is just not on the cards. Only crude planning requires *management*; sophisticated planning is perfectly compatible with wide degrees of freedom. The prospect of "planning for diversity and choice" (to invoke the title of a recent book)[5] is a positive prospect and a definite possibility.

We shall have to consider in substantially greater detail this matter of the welfare involvements of the state. But first attention must be given to another issue. The budgetary aspect of welfare provision as involving the deployment of social resources brings into prominence the political dimension of the welfare problem. After all, the question of what a society is to spend its resources on is the key issue of the political domain. A discussion by Daniel Bell puts into sharp relief the connections operative here:

The irony is that the more planning there is in a society, the more there are open group conflicts. Planning sets up a specific locus of decision, which becomes a visible point at which pressures can be applied. Communal coordination—the effort to create a social choice out of a discordance of individual personal preferences—necessarily *sharpens* value conflicts. . . . [In the case of a single policy] on whose importance and priority the society, by and large, is agreed, there may be little conflict. But what about situations, such as social or welfare policy, where there may be less agreement: how then does one decide? Do we want compensatory education for Negroes at the expense, say, of places for other students when the number of positions is limited? Do we want to keep a redwood forest or provide a going industry to a local com-

5. Stanford Anderson, ed., *Planning for Diversity and Choice* (Cambridge, Mass., 1968). Many parts of this book—the proceedings of a conference "concerned with the improvement of architectural education in the United States"—are relevant to the themes of the present chapter.

138   :   Welfare

munity? . . . These, and thousands more, are issues which cannot be settled on the basis of technical criteria; inevitably they involve value and political choices.[6]

It is high time to consider the political ramifications of the problem of social welfare.

2. Welfare and the Political Process

Since the allocation of public resources to particular programs in pursuit of specified social objectives—public assistance to augment personal finances, publicly financed health or educational programs, etc.—is at issue, the politics of social decision is a decisive factor in regard to public welfare. Collective social action to meet the needs of people is obviously a political issue. The political process is, after all, the preeminent instrumentality by which a society most effectively can and most generally does pursue its public-welfare objectives.

The critical question in this area is, What sorts of political arrangements are best suited to the realization of the welfare objectives of a society? Or, putting the matter with somewhat different emphasis, What political structures can be presumed most responsive to the wishes of a group that accords high priority to realization of the collective welfare? Which political arrangements for social decision-making are most likely to provide guarantees for group welfare?

On first thought, these questions might seem almost trivial, since it would appear that immediate and obvious answers are to be given in terms of *the democratic process.* "Surely," it might be thought, "there can be no way of settling issues concerning the general welfare that can be more effective, or more equitable, than the democratic process of voting as individuals or (when matters of scale make this impossible) through representatives. Voting, after all, is a procedure for arriving at a collective group position on the basis of the expressed wishes of that group's individual members. And since everyone is mindful of his own welfare, noth-

6.   Daniel Bell, "Notes on the Post-Industrial Society (II)," *The Public Interest,* 7 (Spring 1967), pp. 102-18.

ing could be better fitted to provide for the welfare interests of all than a procedure that takes into account the wishes of each." Alas, the matter is not quite so simple. It takes but a brief reexamination of some lines of thought already presented to bring out the fallaciousness of this position.

One well-known theoretical shortcoming of democratic procedures may be characterized as the problem of the *ineffectual minority*. Consider, for example, a society of five members, A through E, assumed to be in an equal position in all relevant respects and confronted by the choice between two alternative policies or programs (labeled I and II), which would result in the following distributions of gains and losses:

	Alternative I	Alternative II
(A)	+3	+2
(B)	+3	+2
(C)	+3	+2
(D)	−5	+3
(E)	−5	+3

If the choice between these two alternative measures were determined by a straight vote, it must be presumed that alternative I would win by a three to two majority; as compared with number II, three persons fare better, two worse. Yet it is quite clear that the "interests of the community" are better served by alternative II. (Forgetting about the societally irrelevant matter of specifically *who* gets a given share, number I has the profile +3, +3, +3, −5, −5 of gain-loss distribution, and number II the profile +3, +3, +2, +2, +2; at the modest cost of substituting one two-unit gain for a three-unit gain, alternative II converts two five-unit losses into two-unit gains.) Thus in this plausible (though, to be sure, artificial) example, persons D and E constitute the "ineffectual minority" whose participation in the voting process is unable to shift its outcome to a socially and patently more desirable result. Moreover, the force of the example is not dependent upon direct rather than representative voting being at issue: we could just as well be dealing with *groups* and the votes of their parliamentary representatives.

Notwithstanding such *theoretical* shortcomings of the democratic process as an instrument for settling issues of general welfare, it must nonetheless be recognized that there are substantial *practical* considerations militating in its favor. One can plausibly question whether *any* reasonable political instrumentality for public decision-making can possibly *guarantee* the optimal realization of group welfare. More positively, the historical realities certainly indicate that the democratic process is in fact quite responsive to the requirements of the general welfare—far more so than any other well-tried alternative. While there are no grounds for holding that a democratic electorate *must*, in the inevitable nature of things, act in the best interests of the general welfare, there is much historical evidence to suppose that, under ordinary circumstances, they will, in actual fact, tend to do so within reasonable limits. Since people are generally motivated to consult their welfare interests, the democratic process does at least go some way toward providing a working mechanism for bringing these elements of the common welfare substantially—even if imperfectly—into play.

Explicit recognition of the theoretical shortcomings of the democratic process is thus by no means tantamount to arguing for its abandonment. Let it be admitted that representative democracy affords no inevitable guarantee of public welfare. Still, there are features of the democratic system as it has come to be operative in contemporary circumstances in advanced societies that render it especially responsive to the demands of welfare. In this light the most reasonable stance is certainly not to argue for the *abandonment* of democratic procedures as a means for resolving issues of general welfare, but rather to argue for their *improvement*. Given an electorate well equipped in point of information, enlightened in its internalizing of the interests of others, and realistic in its assessment of operational feasibilities, the fate of the general welfare can without question be left to the workings of the instrumentalities of democracy.[7]

7. For a vivid and informative discussion of the actualities of the American political process as it bears upon the tug and haul for welfare through the workings

This line of thought calls for somewhat fuller development. There is, in fact, good reason to expect the democratic process to prove substantially efficient and effective in serving the interests of the general welfare whenever the following complex of special conditions obtains:

1. *The condition of valuation of welfare*: The society places a realistically high value upon welfare as a desideratum. Specifically, its members in general exhibit an enlightened and rational self-interest with respect to their own welfare.

2. *The condition of internalization of social welfare*: The society's members have, to some extent, internalized the general welfare as an element in their personal welfare, having a humane sympathy with respect to the welfare of others and a sufficient degree of urbanity and civilized detachment to accept occasional and warranted subordination of their own welfare interests to those of the group and of their interests of the moment to those of the long run.[8]

3. *The condition of informedness*: The society is, in general, informed with reasonable fullness and accuracy as to the actual facts of the case when matters of public welfare are concerned.

4. *The condition of realism*: The members of the society by and large have a realistic appreciation of the extent to which existing circumstances allow for the promotion of their welfare interests. The electorate must be rational, as well as properly informed, regarding the sorts of public-welfare measures that can be achieved. In particular, it is realistic about what the economic base of the society is able to provide and does not espouse an unworkable level of aspiration.

5. *The condition of cohesiveness*: There is, in general, a reasonable consensus within the society regarding the fundamental objectives of public policy, so that a rational pursuit of welfare objectives is not impeded by emotional and divisive side issues.

---

of pressure groups, see Mancour Olson, Jr., *The Logic of Collective Action* (Cambridge, Mass., 1965; reprint ed., New York, 1968).

8. To internalize the welfare interests of others is, of course, to make reference not only to other contemporaries but to posterity as well. The multigenerational time horizon inherent in most measures of social policy is definitely applicable in the sphere of social welfare.

When these five conditions are fulfilled by a society, there are excellent grounds, in the light of recent experiences in nations throughout the world, for expecting that no alternative means for transacting the political business of a society will improve upon the democratic process as a means of assuring feasibly adequate provision for the general welfare. The system of *representative* democracy is particularly congenial to an effective pursuit of the general welfare, because welfare is less a matter of "what people want" than of "what people need." This is as much the case with a society as with an individual, for wants can, of course, stand in overt conflict with welfare interests. At this point, the issues of social engineering, of administrative sagacity, and especially of public education gain enormous importance.[9] In this connection, a passage from the economist T. C. Schelling provides useful insight:

As an economist I have to keep reminding myself that consumer sovereignty is not just a metaphor and is not justified solely by reference to the unseen hand. It derives with even greater authority from another principle of about the same vintage, "no taxation without representation." Welfare economics establishes the convenience of consumer sovereignty and its compatibility with economic efficiency; the sovereignty itself is typically established by arms, martyrdom, boycott, or some principles held to be self-evident. And it includes the inalienable right of the consumer to make his own mistakes.[10]

Yet this line of thought must be counterbalanced by another: that public welfare can at times conflict with the rights of an individual, not his *legal* rights (the way is all too readily paved there) but those he *ought* to have on ethical or moral grounds. There is a critical need, especially in a crowded, urbanized society, for preserving an environment of generally desirable proportions—involving the control of criminals, the maintenance of peace and quiet, the suppression of public nuisances, the support of public health, and

9. For an interesting development of the issues that arise in this connection, see David Braybrooke, *Three Tests for Democracy: Personal Rights, Human Welfare, Collective Preference* (New York, 1968).

10. T. C. Schelling, "The Life You Save May Be Your Own," *Proceedings of the Second Conference on Governmental Expenditures*, Brookings Institution Publication (Washington, D.C., September 15-16, 1966), pp. 127-76, quote from p. 161.

the like. In the interests of shaping a viable common environment, the rights of each individual must be circumscribed by those of his fellows. Throughout the domain of political philosophy run the two key threads of "the general good" and "the right of the individual," sometimes reenforcing each other, sometimes in creative tension, sometimes in outright opposition that verges on destructive conflict. Many difficulties arising in connection with the general welfare are but a specific manifestation of this generic phenomenon.

In traditional liberal democratic theory, *the state* has generally been cast in the role of an intrusive villain against whom the individual must be protected. The key problem is seen as one of establishing the recognition and defense of the rights of the individual against the overriding power of an encroaching state. But one should stress that these considerations—however valid—have been in large measure superseded by others. Nowadays, the principal threat to the individual's rights frequently, nay, even generally, comes *not from the state but from his fellows.* In a crowded mass society whose form of governance is reasonably democratic, the threat to the security of the individual comes in large measure from other individuals in his environment: the criminal, the insane, the boorish, the careless or heedless, etc. There is substantial evidence, for example, that several thousand Americans each year use the automobile as a means of suicide and in many cases "take someone along."[11] In such contexts the individual looks to the state not as an antagonist to his rights but as an indispensable ally in their maintenance. In a democratic social order where the state has been "tamed" and broken to the leash of public needs, the state assumes an increasingly important role in defending an individual against those of his fellows whose actions threaten his welfare interests in myriad ways in the circumstances of contemporary society and technology—ways that do not necessarily call for deliberate malice but may merely involve perfectly inadvertent mischief (as with air and water pollution). This *protective* function of the state is bound to be increasingly prominent as a political aspect of welfare in the future.

11. "Autocide," *Time*, March 10, 1967, p. 23.

A modern society is a very intricate, complex and delicate self-maintaining system or rather constellation of systems in various diverse spheres: the political, economic, medical, and educational. In such macroscopic systems, as with all systems familiar on a smaller scale, there can be *operating malfunctions* over which the individuals involved have relatively little control, but which can work substantially against their common interest. (Think, for example, of a traffic jam.) Under these circumstances the individual looks to the agencies of the state to assure the smooth functioning of these systems upon which virtually every aspect of his welfare is in some way critically dependent.

In considering group welfare as a political objective, it is appropriate to emphasize again a point previously made in several contexts: recognition of the inherently partial and incomplete nature of welfare. For the general welfare, in the short or the long run, is only one among other political values whose pursuit affords the governing objectives of a nation—values such as national independence; security; respect by self and others; and achievement in the pursuit of science, learning, and the arts, excellence in whose cultivation is a significant aim of any self-respecting, civilized nation.

Some, of course, will argue that welfare lies at the bottom of it all and that the sole basis of all other legitimate national objectives is to be seen in their contributions to the general welfare (perhaps only in the long run). Such thinking hovers somewhere in the region of naïveté and self-delusion. Take just one example. The realization of the national aspirations of a people no doubt confers significant benefits upon them, but even a superficial awareness of developments in the "emergent" nations suffices to indicate that this realization need by no means redound to the benefit of the *welfare* of the individuals involved. Again, national achievements in the cultural sphere of the arts and sciences are objectives whose pursuit evokes our respect and whose realization calls forth our admiration. But one need not belong to the school of "art for art's" or "learning for learning's" sake to recognize that even major achievements in these areas may make only minor contributions to the general welfare. In plain fact, there is no warrant for treating the various values operative in the setting of political goals as derivative from welfare. To do so is to espouse unjustifiably a kind of welfare imperialism. For the fact is that other political values are by nature not subordinate to welfare but represent authentic values in their own right. A national society has a legitimate interest in the whole spectrum of these values: its sociopolitical value complex exhibits a *multidimensional* pattern, not a *hierarchical* one where everything depends on welfare.

The opposite extreme also finds its adherents, as with every opposition in social philosophy. Countering those who regard the social welfare as the be-all and end-all of legitimate social concern are those who view any preoccupation with welfare as basically misguided. It is obvious that it is not the "responsible" thinkers of our society who take this line but the critics and opponents of all social orthodoxy: the "irresponsible" avant-garde for whom the cultivation of hedonistic immediacies means everything and the enhancement of stable and long-range resources means nothing. The gilded youth of an affluent society, dismissing—or is it taking for granted?—the factors of welfare (health, material resources, etc.), downgrade or reject welfare as a social goal because it conflicts with what for them is the really important business of *carpe diem*. Scorning the conception of social rationality as economists and other social theorists of the "establishment" have come to view it, they reject the whole social-engineering approach guiding the pursuit of the welfare interests of advanced societies. How the affairs of such a society are to be conducted in a satisfactory way minus this rationality, given the obstacles created by modern technology and demography, is an issue that is not likely to trouble those for whom the very term "responsibility" is pejorative. None the less, running through this entire line of criticisms, there is a useful and valuable thread: it is certainly not legitimate to view welfare and the more or less material issues revolving about it as the sole, or even the major, items on the social agenda. The radically critical position in view can thus serve an eminently constructive purpose if it is taken as making a case not for dismissing welfare, but for merely removing it from a pedestal as the sole or prime social desideratum.

There are no substantial grounds for regarding the general welfare as more than just one among several factors in constituting the goal framework appropriate to a political system. The history of ethical systems in philosophy is full of monolithic *summum bonum* theories to the effect that "*the* objective" of the good life is happiness or knowledge or virtue, etc. But all these "answers" are merely simplistic thinking: what is obviously wanted here is a *balance* among several desiderata. And exactly the same situation obtains in the sphere of social polity. There is no justification for viewing the general welfare as the sole and exclusively predominant objective of political action in public or national affairs; many other factors certainly can and should come into the picture. To deny this is to fall into that simplistically monolithic *summum bonum* thinking characteristic of the doctrinaire and dogmatic political philosophies so greatly in vogue in the nineteenth century.[12]

---

12. Valuable discussions of political aspects of welfare against the background of wider issues of political philosophy are given in three recent books: S. I. Benn and R. S. Peters, *Social Principles and the Democratic State* (London, 1959); Brian Barry, *Political Argument* (London, 1965); and Braybrooke, *Three Tests for Democracy*. It is still useful to consider such contemporary discussions against the classical statements of the traditional-liberalist position in John Stuart Mill's tract, *Essay on Liberty* (London, 1859); and Herbert Spencer's *Social Statics* (London, 1851).

NINE

Beyond the Welfare State

1. The Welfare State

THE GENERALLY ACCEPTED CONCEPTION of the proper task and function of the state has gradually undergone a vast transformation over the past century. Historically, the main duty of the state was first and primarily seen to lie in its *security* functions. Internal and external security (the protection of the country against a hostile menace from abroad and the maintenance of public order within) have traditionally been viewed as the prime tasks of the state. These functions were unrivaled in universal recognition as the unquestionably prime missions of the state in most Western industrial nations throughout the period of what might be called the era of the traditional or the *security state*, certainly covering the period from the French Revolution until the First World War.

As an aftermath of the economic upheavals that followed World War I, culminating in the American Great Depression of the 1930s, a substantial reassessment of the duties of the state came about. During this era, the work of the state was no longer conceived predominantly—nay, almost exclusively—in terms of security; the economic sector now came into prominence. Throughout the Western world, the idea of the *economic* mission of the state came more and more emphatically to the fore. By the mid-1930s the conception of the *full-employment state* was beginning to take a firm hold in Europe and North America. There was substantial agreement and emphatic stress upon the idea that one major function of a state

147

is to assure that its economy is capable of providing a sufficiency of jobs at an adequate level of wages to provide a livelihood for its labor force. The key achievement of the full-employment state was to move the state squarely into the economic arena under the banner of Keynesianism—"depression economics," as it has been called.

A profound shifting of public attitudes accompanied this altered view of the proper mission of the state. In the seventeenth and eighteenth centuries, clear limits came to be defined to restrict interference by governmental authorities with the dealings of private persons. (Recall the sacred rights of life, liberty, and property, as stressed by Locke, that play so critical a role in the great public documents of the founding of the United States.) Nineteenth-century liberal thinkers of the stamp of John Stuart Mill and Herbert Spencer translated these views into a settled doctrine that cast the state in the role of a villain whose wicked machinations will—unless constantly watched and held in check—endanger the rights and liberties of the individual. But this view was increasingly rejected. With the rise of public dependence upon the state as a counterweight to the potentially harmful workings of the economic process, the organs of government were seen to act in a much more benign role. The state came to be seen less and less as a dangerous and hostile—albeit indispensable—intruder in the private affairs of men: it was regarded increasingly as a benign and helpful force for the promotion of the economic necessities of its citizens.

But once the state came to be viewed in this light, why should the matter end here, within the boundaries of certain strictly economic issues? The *welfare state* took definite shape in the wake of the Second World War and the growing economic affluence that became in varying degrees pervasive throughout the West. The transsecurity mission of the state now came to be conceived not merely as calling for the promotion of a healthily functioning "full-employment" economy, but also as making adequate social provisions for all, and especially those groups—such as the young, the ill, the aged, and the various categories of the "chronically poor"— that somehow qualify as "helpless" and unable to participate directly in the fruits of even a thriving economy.

To this point we have considered the matter in terms of something like an evolutionary sequence in which the security state yielded to the full-employment state, which in turn was succeeded by the welfare state. But of course a historical typology of this sort has gross defects. No rigid sequence of neatly separable stages is at issue in this periodization. For one thing, the factors at issue are not really sequential: the security functions of the state have survived—indeed expanded—throughout; the full-employment objective continues to be prominent in the welfare state. We are not talking about stage-by-stage abandonment of old state functions nor of a wholly *ex nihilo* birth of new ones. The focal problems of one phase are never altogether absent in others; it is a matter of the gradual shift into a place of central prominence—and perhaps predominance—of heretofore peripheral issues. It is undoubtedly helpful to cast such an evolutionary process into a sequence of successive stages, but the oversimplifications inherent in this procedure should not be forgotten.

Thus viewed in broad historical retrospect, the welfare state can be seen in terms of a successive broadening of state functions from the traditional core of security (domestic and foreign, public order and defense) to embrace responsibilities first in the economic sphere and then gradually throughout the area of welfare to embrace the medical, the educational, and other sectors. The course of this evolution has seen a progressive deployment of state power over an ever-widening area to provide an acceptable standard of life for the working classes. In certain economies, such as that of Great Britain, provision of adequate goods and services throughout all social strata has not—in the face of limitations of productivity—been possible without significant redistribution. In the United States, however, great productivity has seen an expansion of welfare-state benefits with no substantial redistribution of wealth. But these issues of egalitarianism and redistribution are irrelevant to the core idea of a welfare state as such.

People, Americans especially, frequently tend to think of "the welfare state" under the coloration of *socialism*. But this view sees the matter in a light altogether different from the present perspective. The real issue is not that of state ownership of means of production and state provision of services. As we see it, a welfare state is one which, by whatever means—perhaps only by various financial incentives or by regulatory activities (such as the compulsory purchase of insurances from a private company)—takes upon itself over a wide front the mission of assuring the welfare of its members. Nothing inherent in the concept of social goals that comprises the program of the welfare state requires espousal of the socialistic route to the implementation of the goals, nor indeed is even egalitarianism a necessary consequence. The capitalistic route to the welfare state not only is open but—as recent experience in various countries, including the United States, indicates—can readily be traveled. The zealots of the political Right notwithstanding, America had become by the 1960s certainly not a socialistic state but very definitely a welfare state, in our sense of the term. Here the recognition and implementation of the principle of public responsibility for individual welfare are what count, regardless of the nature of the mechanisms by which this responsibility is met, be they direct state activity or merely state facilitation in creating incentives for the private sector to do the welfare job (e.g., by taxation measures). An adherent to the concept of the welfare state espouses a certain view of the range of a society's responsibilities to its members.

The welfare state as it has evolved in the affluent societies of the West not only has given the welfare of people a place of emphatic prominence, but has, to a significant extent, transformed the conception of what is at issue here. Thus consider the idea of a minimum level of living, the *economic floor* that figured so prominently in the "living wage" of classical economic analysis. In the eighteenth century, it was axiomatic to say of the common workman that, in Turgot's words, "*il ne gagne que sa vie.*" As the society, through the economy that is its productive sector, becomes able to "afford" more and more in the passage from adequacy to abundance, there is an inevitable elevation in the level of expectation of its members, and the levels of "tolerable minimality" are revised drastically upward. The prime task of the welfare state, as it has come to be regarded throughout the West in recent years, is thus best thought of in terms of the concept of *deprivation* or rather the prevention thereof. The welfare state thus secured certain key missions going well beyond the tasks of the full-employment state —above all, the mission of elimination of insufficiency in general and poverty in particular. Unquestionably deprivation has many facets—the educational and medical dimensions and other basic aspects of a satisfactory life all enter in—but economic deprivation is the most prominent and fundamental of these. Thus the eradication of impoverishment has come to represent, at least in theory, a leading, if not *the* leading, social objective of the welfare state. And as compared with the aspirations of the security state and the full-employment state, this desideratum is in significant measure an altogether *new* objective.

The aims of the welfare state of the twentieth century are too familiar to need much elaboration. In fundamental aspect they are essentially defensive matters of protection: safeguarding the individual against falling below some minimal level in his access to essential goods and services. They primarily and principally look to the protection of various categories of persons handicapped in some way or other—dependent children, the ill, the aged, the unemployed, etc.—against the physical and especially the economic hardships created for them by the circumstances of modern society.[1] The resultant characteristics of the modern welfare state are also well known. Everyone is familiar with its general features: the extensive programs of social insurance, unemployment benefits, medical care, public assistance to the needy, etc. All these call for enormous expenditures of public funds, and their administration requires bureaucratic activity on a vast scale, as well as the maintenance of a healthy economy capable of affording the massive costs entailed.

The striking feature of the welfare state is thus its continuation of the preoccupation of its predecessor, the full-employment state, with the economic sector of the society's concerns. Because a technologically advanced modern economy is the sort of thing it is, the welfare state has come to assume certain definite and characteristic forms. As a result, the functioning of the welfare state has become fixed along stylized and specifiable lines. Since its aim is to

1. Harry K. Girvetz in *Encyclopedia of the Social Sciences*, s.v. "Welfare State," see p. 512.

assure (where necessary through the instrumentality of state action) a socially uniform set of minimal standards, the welfare state presents two characteristic features in its actions: comprehensiveness and centralization. The ideals of uniformity of standard and universality of access that lie at the core of the definitive mission of the welfare state make for a concentration of its functions and tend to uniformity and hierarchical monolithism in operational practice.[2] On the one hand, we have seen an enormous expansion and diffusion in the sphere of state activity: a constant broadening of state functions and expansion of its responsibilities. On the other hand, this proliferation of state action has been matched by an awesome centralization of control. As a result, the dominant feature of the operation of the welfare state has been a steady increase in bureaucratic centralism that has manifested itself in every sphere of governmental action, from the gathering of statistics to the administration of the traditional machinery for taxation, law enforcement, etc.

Despite the potential dangers inherent in the mode of operation of the welfare state, dangers which rendered any movement in a welfare-oriented direction anathema from the standpoint of nineteenth-century liberalism, there is no question that the *theory* behind it seems socially benign. In the ideology of the welfare state, the concept of the public good is central and preeminent. It sees this good in terms of certain key objectives: economic welfare; economic, social, and political egalitarianism; the avoidance of deprivation; the diffusion of basic services; and the like. Throughout, there runs a *leitmotiv* of disaster prevention, of safeguarding people against unpleasant eventualities, of avoiding or ameliorating both the absolute and the relative sort of catastrophe that threatens men living in the setting of modern economic conditions.

The benign ideology has, however, tended to give the welfare state a certain negativistic aspect. Its spokesmen have generally evinced a penchant for bottom-oriented thinking, a praiseworthy but in some ways depressing preoccupation with improving the lot of the deprived and underprivileged. Their theme has tended

2. Experimentalism and variety are consequently enormously difficult to realize in this context.

to work itself out in terms of catastrophe prevention rather than life-enhancement, of protection against hazards rather than the realization of opportunities. The welfare state became the repository of the earlier tradition of private charity and paternalistic concern for "the less fortunate" that characterized the higher-minded among the privileged classes of the older social order.

The strengths of the welfare state are substantial. The *standard of living* has been the motto emblazoned upon its banner and great things have been achieved in its name. Its dangers are perhaps equally well known: the centralization of power and control; the evolution of the "Big Brother" state, paternalistic in intent, but authoritarian in operation; the approaching era of the "universal data bank" and pervasive social engineering—curtailing privacy, initiative, and the sphere of effective operation of individual effort. But even before these essentially political threats of the welfare state stands the economic weakness it has displayed on its home ground: the signal failure to realize its own professed objectives. For it is beginning to be clear (being amply documented, for example, in Michael Harrington's *The Other America*) that the modern measures of economic welfare have failed to penetrate through to the bottom rungs of the economic ladder and so to reach those who have most need of such measures. The charge has been made —and well supported—that the welfare state has in practice been deplorably ineffectual in benefiting those who most need it: the groups at the very bottom of the economic heap who have for practical purposes been disenfranchised, politically and socially, as well as economically. And not only have the utterly deprived been stepchildren of the welfare state, but also they have been the workers of the lowest category. They have had to watch with impotence and frustration as wage differentials with higher-paid endeavors have in fact increased, rather than lessened, in a system that claims to aim at an escalation of minima and a leveling of differences.

The expansion of the welfare state has also been accompanied by a substantial series of unfortunate (and unintended) "side effects" in the sphere of human values. Now that the children of what might be called the welfare-state generation born after

World War II—reared, in substantial part, under conditions of relative affluence—are reaching maturity, these malign effects are becoming increasingly discernible. These value-related upheavals include such items as:

1. An unrealistic devaluation of economic security as such (by depreciation in the wake of realization)

2. The erosion of initiative (the "man in the gray flannel suit"; rise of testing and counseling)

3. The flight from responsibility ("let George do it"; Miss Genovese and the twenty-seven witnesses)

4. The growing ambivalence to authority (increasing dependence thereon and resentment thereof)

5. Rising expectations (possible unrealism with inherent danger of social discontent and upheaval)

6. The rise of ambivalence to physical comfort (growing dependence, but dislike to admit it)[3]

Such value reactions have tended to make themselves felt throughout the citizenry of the welfare state. But other effects have become concentrated among those who are the recipients of extensive public assistance. Primary among these is a weakening of the spirit of self-help and self-reliance which at its worst can slip into a condition of impotent, near fatalistic dependency. Other sad consequences follow from the condescension often present among those who administer public-assistance programs, creating an uncooperative, depressed, apathetic outlook. The resultant "culture of welfarism" creates an unvital, pathological climate of attitude and opinion where effective self-help is impossible. As an instrumentality for escaping from the depressed ethos of the urban ghetto, the American Negro has turned to the path of widespread revolt and anger, including thoughtful protest on the part of some and simply antisocial conduct on that of others. Apparently this way alone has offered a means to break the attitudinal bonds that welfarism has created among its beneficiaries.[4]

3. For a further discussion of the relevant issues, see my essay "What is Value Change?" in *Values and the Future*, eds. K. Baier and N. Rescher (New York, 1969).

4. For an illuminating development of this theme, see Frank Riessman, *Strategies Against Poverty* (New York, 1967).

From this standpoint, it would seem that the way in which the welfare state has evolved in the American setting has rendered it a definitely mixed blessing. For in this context the welfare state has in many ways failed to realize its own professed objectives—for example, as we saw in the discussion of poverty. Moreover, its positive improvement of the lot of many individuals has been accompanied by unfortunate—and frequently unforeseen—side effects of various kinds. Such negative aspects of the welfare state give particular point to the question of its prospects for the future.

The preoccupation of the welfare state with economic themes relating to the avoidance of individual-afflicting disasters makes it plausible to view it as grappling with the problems of a transient era. After all, the avoidance of economic catastrophe and the safeguarding of "the man at the bottom" are relatively attainable goals—as the manifest successes of the welfare state would indicate. An economy that is adequately productive and adequately egalitarian would dismantle, or at any rate transform, much of the machinery of the welfare state by reaching a point where people can, or with an added modicum of egalitarian redistribution could, perfectly well attend to their personal-welfare needs. Correspondingly, one anticipates an era—and in affluent countries it could prove to be not a distant one—when the welfare state will have "worked itself out of a job" by effectually discharging its mission.[5] One can look forward from this perspective toward the time when the welfare state will have seen its day and give way to a successor. But what sorts of issues can be expected to be at the center of the public agenda of this postwelfare state?

2. *Social Goals Beyond Welfare*

The previous section depicted the welfare state as a transitory phenomenon. Designed to deal with what are, in effect, the eco-

---

5. This view, of course, might seem drastically overoptimistic in the absence of qualifications. For the advanced countries of Europe, North America, and Australia, "normal" conditions and the absence of major wars may well be sufficient presuppositions; while with other, less-advanced nations a great deal more must be assumed in terms of an absence of local "limited" conflicts, the control of population expansion, and even, in some cases, a restructuring of the social order.

nomic problems of a specific era, as well as the social and political issues that revolve about them, the welfare state appears to be in the process of giving way to its successor. This we might call, for want of a more elegant name, the postwelfare state. As its very designation suggests, the objectives that confront this evolutionary successor of the welfare state will, in the main, be found to lie outside the welfare orbit. But what might these objectives be? To answer this question we must explore the province of social desiderata that transcend the traditional area of welfare.

Much of the previous discussion has been devoted to clarifying the nature of welfare. For present purposes, however, it is necessary to reexamine welfare in a critical light, confronting the question of its limitations and boundaries. Above all, the issue of social goals *beyond* welfare deserves careful consideration. Only against this preparatory background will it be fruitful to consider whether the welfare-centered society represents an ultimate ideal or is to be viewed as an interim point on the road to other no less significant objectives.

It is obviously appropriate and desirable that an *individual* should have life goals that extend beyond his own welfare and that of his kindred. When one contemplates the range of the desirable achievements and accomplishments of a person, it appears that most of them do not lie within the restricted confines of welfare. Only a rather narrow band of the broad spectrum of human values falls into the region of welfare, whereas most values of significance fall outside. A man's aesthetic and contemplative values, for example, his being educated (along other than minimal or vocational lines), his taking an intelligent interest in the arts, or his pursuit of enjoyable avocations, are not matters that affect his welfare but do all the same represent important human desiderata.[6] Nor are the pleasures of life necessarily to be located in the welfare area. Of the seven deadly sins (pride, greed [covetousness], lust, anger, gluttony, envy, and sloth) at most three—namely, greed, lust, and

---

6. For a general survey of the sphere of values, see N. Rescher, *Introduction to Value Theory* (New York, 1969), especially chap. 2. Some specific discussion of the place of social welfare as a value is given in the second chapter of the present volume.

gluttony—have a direct and immediate connection with material welfare. Welfare is certainly important but it is also incomplete. When one examines the constituent components of "the good" for a man, one finds this to encompass many things that lie outside the area of his welfare.

The case with regard to social welfare is exactly analogous. Social groups can and do, quite legitimately, assume for themselves not only welfare objectives but nonwelfare ones as well. Welfare has to do with the material requisites for a satisfying life, but this very focus on the material is the clear sign of the limited and restricted scope of this whole issue of welfare. A people can have a good standard of living, possessing material prosperity, a satisfactory state of public health, etc., and yet be lacking in education, culture, artistic and scientific creativity, and the good manners and decencies that make for civilized life. The standard of living is only one among many elements of public well-being, even as material comfort (however broadly understood) is only one among many elements of personal well-being. The members of a society whose welfare is in a salubrious condition can all the same lead a low, demeaned, and in many respects impoverished existence. To set up welfare as the supreme political goal is narrow-minded folly. Thus while welfare, like security, may well indicate the prime needs of an era, it scarcely qualifies as a social ultimacy. The biblical dictum that "man does not live by bread alone" can be applied to welfare also. (Though, of course, this is not to say that he who lacks bread, or other requisites of welfare, is in a position to devote himself to these other matters.) To say all this is not to downgrade welfare but to recognize that as a human desideratum it is not the be-all and end-all, but simply one leading element which, along with many others, forms part of a complex composite.

For the individual person there are, or, as we have seen, certainly should be, important goals beyond welfare, goals whose attainment, or even pursuit, makes for a happier or perhaps even a better person. Examples of such goals include attainment of the respect of his associates and the love of some among them; pride of achievement in some areas of activity, vocational or avocational; appreciation of the attainments of the race in art and science; the enjoyment of hobbies or sports; etc. These goals all revolve about the theme of self-development and fulfillment, a capitalizing upon the opportunities for the realization of a man's potential for appreciating and contributing to the creative impetus of the human spirit. The achievement of such goals lays the basis for a legitimate view of oneself as a unit of worth: a *person* in the fullest sense. And a significant and general lack in these regards is indicative, not necessarily of any diminution of welfare, but of an impoverishment of spirit. In consequence, people as individuals have (i.e., can, should, and do have) a wide spectrum of *transwelfare goals*: goals the attainment of or progress toward which is definitely to be viewed as broadly speaking "in the interest" of a person, although his *welfare* might not specifically suffer from their lack. In a wholly parallel way, there are legitimate goals for a society that extend well beyond the region of the welfare of its members: in the cultivation of literary, artistic, and scientific creativity and appreciation, etc.; in the forging of an attractive and comprehensively *pleasant* life-environment; in the cultivation of congeniality in human interactions; in preserving and enhancing the appreciation of our historical, cultural, and intellectual heritage, etc.

For societies, as for individuals, *transwelfare goals count*: they have a validity, legitimacy, and importance all their own. Since the heyday of utilitarianism in the first part of the nineteenth century, the thesis that maximization of personal pleasure and its composite cousin, general welfare, is the ultimate pivot of social philosophy has gained widespread currency, even to the point of attaining the status of an established dogma. To adopt this view, however, is to overlook something very basic: the inherent incompleteness of welfare. Welfare gains its great importance as a human objective from its concern with the minimalities of a satisfactory life, but this very source of its importance marks its insufficiency as well. Beyond welfare there lies not only the hedonic sector of human enjoyment but also, and most significantly, the whole aristic sector of man's higher goals and aspirations.

No matter how we shape in its details our overarching vision of the good life for man, welfare will play only a partial and subsidiary role because a satisfactory condition of affairs as to welfare is compatible with a substantial impoverishment outside the region of welfare minima. Indeed, a person, or a society, can be healthy, prosperous, and literate, but yet lack all those resources of personality, intellect, and character which, like cultivation of mind and fostering of human congeniality, make life rewarding as well as pleasant. (Think again of Mill's dictum, "Better to be Socrates dissatisfied than a pig satisfied.") A society can and should look beyond the physically comfortable life comprising its welfare to the fostering of those conditions and circumstances that make for the conditions in which life can be rich, full, and rewarding. The material factors at issue in welfare are only the springboard from which a society can move on to other, more deeply meaningful objectives. It can—and should—care not only for the standard of living of its people but for their cultural development, for example, and indeed even for "the good name and fame" of the group.

Toward people or nations who have—even to abundance—the constituents of welfare, we may well feel envy, but our *admiration* and *respect* could never be won on this ground alone. An entire dimension of legitimate human desiderata lies beyond welfare, indeed even beyond the realm of happiness as such. For there are many things which give people *satisfaction*—perfectly legitimate satisfaction—without rendering them any *happier*. The reader of biographies cannot but become convinced that there are full and satisfying lives—eminently worthwhile lives—that are not particularly happy, but shot through with that "quiet desperation" that Thoreau perhaps mistakenly imputes to most men. And contrariwise, there are happy lives that are deplorable and may well be so deemed (quite rightly) by the persons who "enjoy" them. My aim, however, is not to dwell on these lugubrious facets of the human situation, but to stress one relatively simple and straightforward point: that any adequate vision of "the good life" for people—and for societies—must reckon with areas of human achievement wholly outside the welfare area. Neither for individuals nor for societies is "the pursuit of happiness" the sole and legitimate guide to action; its dictates must be counterbalanced by recognizing the importance of doing those things upon which in after years we can look back with justifiable pride.

The central concept of this excellence-connected, transwelfare domain is *quality*, particularly in the realization of human potentialities: in actual creativity, in the appreciation thereof, and in the forging of rewarding human interrelationships. Excellence, dignity, and the sense of worth are the leading themes throughout. Here we have left behind the domain of the minima at issue with welfare to enter another sphere—that of human ideals relating to man's higher and nobler aspirations. Clearly, a civilized society has an important stake not only in the area of welfare and its hedonistic ramifications but in this "higher" region as well. A civilized social order must, of course, concern itself with the needs of its people for the requisites of happiness, but it must also look to the area of excellence—excellence in creativity, in appreciation, and in fostering the realization of human potential. At an early point—well before it reaches even minimal levels of affluence—a civilized society can no longer defensibly content itself merely with putting a welfare floor under people through the implementation of minimalistic standards (however escalated): its vision must reach beyond these limits altogether. Any truly civilized society owes it to itself—and to its posterity—to support the creation and appreciation of positive human achievement in science, learning, the arts, sports, and in sum in all areas of creative human activity where the concept of excellence is operative.[7]

This points to an enlarged view of "the social good" that goes every bit as far outside the area of social welfare as any traditional view of "the good life" for man goes beyond the basics of individual welfare. On this view, a civilized society comes to qualify as such only when it devotes some reasonable proportion of its human and material resources to the cultivation of the fields of human excellence. This concept of "the social good" requires that a significant place be given to the instrumentalities of culture and human cultivatedness: the arts, the institutions of research and higher education, the restoration and preservation of antiquities,

7. A useful discussion of some facets of the role in contemporary American society of individual excellence and individual creativity is given in B. M. Gross and M. Marien, "The President's Questions and Some Answers" in *A Great Society?* ed. B. M. Gross (New York, 1966), pp. 3-31; see esp. pp. 18-23.

etc. With societies and nations, as with individuals, a balanced goal structure calls for a proportionate recognition of *the domestic impetus* concerned with the welfare well-being of people, with home and hearth, stomach and pocketbook, good fellowship, rewarding work, etc. But it also calls for recognition of *the heroic impetus* concerned with the recognition of ideals, creative achievements, playing a significant role on the world-historical stage, and doing those splendid things upon which posterity looks with admiration—above all the winning of battles: not those of the battlefield but those of the human mind and spirit.

What, after all, do we, as external observers, view as deserving of respect in our scrutiny of other societies? Think of spelling out the standards one is inclined to apply here—standards among which a reference to creative achievement is prominently operative. A society does not sustain these tests unless it is prepared to invest some ample share of its resources in the cultivation of goals outside the boundaries of welfare. This perspective has a deep-rooted source. The imposition of order on chaos—intellectual, social, environmental—is a central and continuous theme of human history. In that light what we find admirable in a society is the *quality* of its life both as this relates to the pattern of day-to-day life (along the line of works dealing with *Everyday Life in Ancient Babylonia*) and also as it relates to a society's creative achievement.

The efforts made in this direction should be proportionate to the means of the society, but it is crucial that they be made, and made, however modestly, in a way that exhibits some roughly appropriate balance. A modern society without its historians and its poets —nay, even its Egyptologists—suffers a kind of spiritual malnutrition. The criteria for assessing any civilized society call for close scrutiny not only of its standard of living but of its achievements as well. The society that starves its culture must be ranked with that of boors, savages, and barbarians.

But what justifies this insistence that society recognize the claims of excellence? Certainly not an appeal to social welfare: it smacks of brazen hypocrisy to argue that maintenance of art galleries, botanical gardens, or the classical stage somehow advance the *welfare* of people. If the allocation of substantial social resources to museums, symphony orchestras, or institutes of advanced studies is justified—as I am convinced it is—the justification cannot proceed on the basis of welfare advancement; it should not be given with reference to *welfare* at all (no matter how indirect), but given, rather, in terms of something else that is just as important: an *investment in social ideals.* For the very having of ideals, values, and aspirations is patently a critical social desideratum.

As the achievement of comfort is not enough for a person, so the realization of the public welfare is not enough for a society. Even as a person is right to concern himself not only with his welfare, with his *self-realization*, with "what he makes of himself" and "what sort of life he leads," so a society has—on the moral side—an inalienable obligation to foster the *quality* of its collective life. A person can realize his highest potential only when he "sets his sights" on goals that go far beyond issues relating to his standard of living. Similarly in society, the pursuit of the "higher" goals is fundamentally important. This is something in which every member of the society has a stake—albeit a *nonwelfare* stake. For the individual this is a matter of self-image, self-realization, self-identity, and just plain pride. The citizen of a nation that does not neglect its duties in this area can say to himself proudly, "I am one of those men who were in the vanguard of attaining this or that frontier of human achievement, one of those who produce the best mountaineers or sea captains of the world, one of those who first pushed the actualization of human potential toward some higher plateau in the realization of justice or the advancement of knowledge or artistic creation." What is at issue here is not a utilitarian defense in terms of welfare benefits to people but a defense in terms of the general principle of human ideals.

No impoverishment of purse is as hurtful as an impoverishment of spirit, and no route more surely leads to this tragic destination than the despising and neglect of the sectors of human achievement which compel admiration even in those of us who only look on from the sidelines. Where welfare is deficient, ideals may well be ineffective, and yet there is at least a stimulus to improvement. But welfare without ideals is utterly corruptive and debilitating. A society that yields up its ideals for the mere betterment of its welfare exchanges its birthright for a mess of pottage.

From this standpoint, it becomes plain what answer is to be given to the question of whether the welfare-centered society is an optimal utopia or whether it has intrinsic weaknesses and short-comings. Concern for welfare is all very well as far as it goes, but welfare is myopic in failing to look outside the range of immediate human needs—perhaps even "needs" that have been very substantially escalated in an affluent society.

To this point we have only considered a handful of somewhat random examples of transwelfare goals. A more systematic consideration of this central issue is desirable, indeed obligatory. Let us proceed once again by an analogy with the situation in the case of the individual. When one views the interests of individuals in the broader perspective of the quality of life, then, as we saw in chapter 4, two sectors outside the welfare area are of special importance:

1. The *hedonic* sector of the more personal and transient enjoyments, embracing those things that enrich life with enjoyment, fun, gaiety, etc.

2. The *aristic* sector of excellence in quality of life, embracing those things that make for a *better person*—even if not necessarily a happier one—by making his life fuller, richer, deeper, etc.

Both these dimensions of individual goals are also operative at the social level. On the aristic side, we encounter everything that relates to the aspect of excellence in activity and achievement. The pertinent examples cover a wide range: original achievement in science, learning, and the arts; the dissemination of products of culture and creativity in museum displays, stage performances, concerts and recitals, etc.; the preservation and public availability of antiquities and of the beauties of nature; etc. This aristic sector deserves emphatic stress. As the pendulum of fashion in social attitudes swings, ours are hedonistic times. The tendency of the day is to worry about making people happier; it is not fashionable to talk of making them better. (We tend, at any rate, to assume this standpoint in our social outlook; at the immediately proximate environment of our own family, the perspective may be different. We want our own immediate connections—parents, spouses, children—to be *both* happy *and* enlightened, good people and would be reluctant to see too much of the latter be traded against gains in the former.) There is at bottom no reason why a social concern for the aristic dimension of life should not accompany that for welfare.

On the other hand, one must also recognize the hedonic dimension of social activity: the realization of the conditions for happiness-conducive individual action in the contexts of social interaction. This includes not only the creation of opportunities for rewarding recreation and the enjoyable use of leisure in conjunction with others, but more generally the realization of pleasantness in the matrix of social transaction: the creation of pleasant operating conditions in all aspects of communal life. In large measure, this is a matter of smoothing the natural frictions of human interaction under the crowded circumstances of modern urban civilization. The aim here is the humanization of man's dealings with man, the fostering of civilizedness, civility, cordiality, and everything that makes for pleasantness in a man's contacts with others. Thus with an entire society as with a single individual, the transwelfare goals are essentially bound up with the realization of human potential. These facets of the quality of life in its public aspect—the social dimension of human excellence, the playful aspect of enjoyment through human sociability in ways going beyond the requirements of welfare, and the realization of pleasantness throughout the area of interpersonal dealings—all represent important groups of social desiderata outside the welfare area. These considerations yield the main outlines of the region of transwelfare objectives on the social (rather than individual) side of the matter.

It might be objected: "Granted that these transwelfare objectives are of value in the long run. But in the here and now, in the short run, they are simply unaffordable luxuries. What concern has a society with the pursuit of transwelfare goals until after the first item of its agenda—the welfare of its members—has been properly attended to?" To this objector we reply that his reasoning is misleading and mistaken. It is (or should be) a familiar fact that there are priorities which simply cannot be translated into *sequences*. A physician cannot tell his patient, "Postpone exercise until your diet has been perfected." It makes no sense to advise a student to put off beginning to learn French until he has perfected his Latin. A society must be prepared to cultivate its pursuit of and taste for excellence and enjoyment even amid material adversity, otherwise both the taste and the capacity for its appeasement will be dead before the day of prosperity arrives. The plant that is not kept living through the winter cannot flourish in the springtime. The *trans*welfare goals cannot be made over into *post*welfare goals because such a (superficially plausible) temporally sequential ordering of priorities would in fact render the ultimate realization of the postponed aim very difficult and perhaps even impossible.

The crass financial implications of these considerations must not be shirked. The fact that realization of a society's transwelfare objectives competes for resources with that of its welfare objective renders *some* conflict inevitable. Money spent on museums, libraries, concert halls, universities, etc., cannot go to funding desirable programs of public assistance. (And it is virtually axiomatic that the financial backing of such programs is never sufficient to the needs.) All the same, this "diversion" of social resources outside the welfare area is certainly justified. Even as important political values such as freedom and justice can conflict with collective welfare, and on occasion should rightly triumph over it, so the furtherance of transwelfare objectives is—even in a poor society— justified to some proportionate extent. Posterity can only enjoy what has survived to reach it: the natural beauties annihilated, the decayed objects of traditionary interest, and the buildings and works of art crumbled into dust are not readily revived. Moreover, it is only through at least *some* cultivation of transwelfare goals that the ideals and aspirations of a society can find the expression they need to maintain themselves as living realities.

Thus insofar as a successor to the welfare state can be expected to occupy itself with human objectives outside the welfare area, there is no lack of work to be done. For the state could then be expected to turn to the truly Herculean task of working toward the transwelfare goals, striving for the creation of a climate of life that is conducive to auspicious patterns of interpersonal relationships and that gives due emphasis to the realization of excellence in human achievement. Having spelled out a frame of reference in which the successor of the welfare state *can* find its mandate, it is perhaps high time to take an explicit look at the postwelfare state itself.

3. The Postwelfare State

The concept of *the postindustrial society* was originally coined by David Riesman[8] to designate the new type of social order emerging as the production of goods becomes a decreasingly significant sector of a highly efficient economy, capable at one and the same time of creating general affluence, providing for increased leisure, and redirecting resources to the production of services (rather than goods). Noting that the transition from the industrial to the postindustrial order matches in importance that from the preindustrial to the industrial, Daniel Bell has striven to win acceptance of this term to indicate the future social order of the technologically advanced societies.[9]

Under the conditions of the postindustrial order, the available productive technology will be such as to yield a substantial increase in the output of goods and services at a significant decrease in the investment of people's time and energy. Though America is as yet only in the early stages of a movement toward this condition and a full-blown postindustrialism will not be reached here— or anywhere—for perhaps a generation or more, the operation of a powerful trend in this direction can already be discerned. This far-reaching development in the socioeconomic order of things carries with it profound implications for the concept of the proper work of the state and correspondingly for the nature of the state itself.

Before our very eyes, a new conception of the work of the state is beginning to take form. There is a growing dissatisfaction with the fact that the welfare state has placed an overemphasis on the economic dimension of life. Consider just one example of this. How

8. David Riesman, "Leisure and Work in Post-Industrial Society" in *Mass Leisure,* eds. E. Larrabee and R. Meyersohn (Glencoe, Ill., 1958).
9. Daniel Bell, *Penguin Survey of the Social Sciences* (London, 1965).

does the welfare state explain and justify its preoccupation with education and the inevitably substantial investment of resources in the educational system? It has tended to do so in strictly economic terms: its youth are part of the economic assets (the "manpower resources") of the nation, and their education provides the pool of highly trained talent needed to make a modern economic system go at full steam. Education, in short, is seen as an instrumentality of economic prosperity. We thus arrive at what might be termed the *economic* justification of education in terms of an investment in "human capital."[10] (Note that this is wholly parallel to the way in which the traditional state tended to justify all measures—economic ones included—by placing them under the umbrella of "national security.") Serious scholars and educators, of course, have never adhered to this way of thinking; theirs is much more of an art-for-art's-sake type of concept, namely, that of education for the sake of intellectual enlightenment or *cultural* enrichment. (This is not to say, of course, that educational administrators have not "played the game" when seeking the financial support of the welfare state.) It is a noteworthy phenomenon of the latter 1960s that the students themselves began increasingly to reject this economic justification of education, refusing to see their education in economic terms as a matter of increasing their economic value and usefulness. This is just one small sign—though a rather significant one—of a growing shift away from the traditionally economic preoccupations of the welfare state.

The welfare state may thus come to be seen with the "wisdom of hindsight" as a transitional order of things, one designed to cope with the social problems and difficulties of an era preceding conditions of economic affluence in a democratically organized postindustrial society. After all, the relative avoidance of catastrophe and the improvement of the lot of "the man at the bottom" are largely—though admittedly never completely—attainable socioeconomic goals. One can thus look hopefully to the onset of a new social era, one not oriented primarily to the avoidance or mitigation of catastrophes but preoccupied with improving the quality

10. Cf. G. S. Becker, *Human Capital*, National Bureau of Economic Research, General Series, no. 80 (New York, 1964).

of life of people in general. Once this prospect of a sociopolitical order of a *postwelfare* variety is realized, the principal item on the social agenda will no longer be the provision of basic needs—however nonminimally these may be conceived of—but rather the creation of conditions conducive to a more favorable climate of life throughout the society. The central preoccupation of the postwelfare state will be not with the implementation of minimal standards, with keeping people "above the floor" of administrative minima in access to goods and services, but with the more positive tasks of forging circumstances that encourage and support people in their efforts "to make the best of themselves."

The successor of the welfare state will differ from it primarily in ways that reflect a fundamental shift in value orientation, a changeover to the view of the central "social problem" as one of forging the setting of a *satisfying* life rather than as one of providing for the minimalities of an *adequate* life. The welfare state has seen its mission in essentially *protective* terms; its preoccupation has been defensive in an endeavor to safeguard people against hazards of various sorts. The postwelfare state will assume a more positive aspect, concerning itself with the transwelfare goals of life enhancement, with the aristic sector coming to increasing prominence. The attitudinal upheaval at issue is not, of course, one of the introduction of wholly new values or the abandonment of old ones, but rather one of a shift in emphasis and of the revision of a scale of political values. The traditional problems of the distributive and—now especially—the collective sectors of welfare will not be left behind by the postwelfare state. But this new order will differ from the welfare state as developed in Britain or Scandinavia—and even in the affluent circumstances of the United States —especially in three ways in regard to its basic value structure.

1.   The prime focus of political emphasis will be shifted away from catering to the basic human needs of the welfare complex to the forging of more pleasant operating conditions for the conduct of life under the crowded circumstances of modern times (especially in the urban centers).

2.   A higher priority will be given to goals of the cultural-creative sector. It will come to be recognized in a more emphatic way

than ever before that society has a commitment to and responsibility for the level of its culture and the appreciation of its cultural heritage, with a correspondingly heightened emphasis on higher education, the development of the arts, etc. Society and its instrumentalities will take increased interest in the institutions dedicated to supporting appreciation of the arts, the preservation of antiquities, etc. There will be a renewed stress on quality, excellence, and creativity and a fostering of opportunities for action and appreciation along these lines.

3. The great surge of nationwide uniformity typical of the mass-orientedness of the welfare state (mass production, mass media, mass politics) will give way to some extent to fragmentation. There will be renewed emphasis on regionalisms, parochialisms, "participatory democracy," and decentralized group action of many sorts, as well as a more strident insistence upon cultural diversity and social fragmentation. In consequence there will be a renewed striving for diversity in unity and cohesiveness in variety. The postwelfare society will seek to combine unity with diversification and to become a whole, embracing highly variegated components (a genuine *unum e pluribus*).

The affluence of the postindustrialized society is an essential precondition of the postwelfare state. And it is, in this context, important to split apart the economists' traditional packaging together of "goods and services." The technology of postindustrialism, by creating a situation where the production of *goods* requires the energies of fewer people, opens up a greater scope for the production of *services*. This service orientation is the key feature of the economy of postwelfare order, because it has become possible to shift the focus of social concern to other than the traditionally "material" needs. The sector of services poses some unique economic problems, because quality services can be rendered only on a man-to-man basis: the doctor can only examine a few patients each day, the barber can only shave one customer at a time, the professor can lecture to throngs but tutor no more than a handful, the actress can provide entertainment for many at once but companionship to only a few. And though there is no effective limit to the quantity of services a man can *consume* (think of the entourage of a monarch), each man can produce only one man-day of personal services per diem. Consequently, a society can never be affluent in quality services in the way in which it can—given automation—become affluent in quality goods: the per capita distribution of quality services is of necessity confined within narrow limits. And yet it is precisely because the problem of the availability of goods is closer to solution in the postindustrial era that that of services now moves to the center of the stage.

The downgrading of traditional economic values in the postindustrial era of affluence thus comes to be matched by a heightened prominence of values relating to such social issues as culture, politics, education, workmanship, and the creative use of leisure. This value reorientation of the postindustrial era has far-reaching implications for the political *modus operandi* of the postwelfare state. The welfare state as it has developed in the European and North American settings is based upon a comprehensive hierarchical bureaucracy and a highly centralized control structure. Unified coordination and control has been virtually inevitable because of the nature of the problems with which the welfare state has been primarily designed to cope. Three factors have been especially significant here:

1. The bulk of the problems confronted by the welfare state have been economic in nature—or at any rate in origin—and a nation's economy lends itself with relative ease to centralized direction and control. (In this regard a nation's economic life stands in contrast to its sociopsychological and its cultural dimensions.)

2. Prominent among the most fundamental problems of the welfare state have been the issues of economic and political egalitarianism. The results of equality and across-the-board equity can clearly and obviously be most efficiently pursued by a centralized uniformitarianism.

3. The issues with which the welfare state has been concerned have been ones that can be tackled effectively by the legislative process. They revolve about issues of control and are thus of such a kind as to be responsive to centralized direction.

By contrast, the critical issues confronting the postwelfare state will be of a different order. The problems that will come to the

fore in the society it serves will, as we have argued, relate largely
or primarily not to the economic sector but to that of the cultural
and sociopsychological. As such, they are most effectively and
naturally amenable to a decentralized treatment better adapted to
accommodate regional and communal differences. In consequence,
most of the structure of the postwelfare state will become multi-
cellular rather than monolithically centralized. The "table of organization" of the many sectors of the postwelfare state will look
like a spider's web rather than an inverted tree. A substantial re-
alignment of the channels in which power and authority run will
be called for, involving a marked localization of control: a shift
away from the pattern of control flowing downward from on high
in the centralized hierarchy toward a relocation of authority in
local units with the resultant creation of instrumentalities conducive to the implementation of local initiative. The individual member of the postwelfare state will have to be much closer—and to
feel much closer—to the effectively operative sources of authority
and control. This is the pattern already to be discerned in a rudimentary way in present trends toward a shift from the bureaucratic centralization of the welfare state to that less monolithic,
more diffused, and increasingly "participatory" democracy that
will be characteristic of its postwelfare successor. In the new
regime, *government* as such may well attain a heretofore undreamt
of importance in institutions at all levels. But there will be a corresponding recognition of not just the *governing* but also the *educational* and *motivational* mission of the functionaries of governing
power.

The welfare state has occupied a unique historical position. The
principal social goals of the era, the main issues on the agenda of
the society (economic growth, economic justice, political and economic egalitarianism, the forging of adequate "social services"),
were such as to be efficiently and effectively handled at the level
of the state. But in the more affluent and socially more complex
environment of the postwelfare state, this circumstance no longer
obtains. The "issues of the day" will in large measure be such as
to lie outside the sphere of effective action at the governmental
level. The state as such will become increasingly less relevant to
the society's problems because it will become increasingly less effi-

cient in coping with them. The society will in consequence have to readjust to ways of achieving its goals other than through the instrumentality of the state.

This is not to say, of course, that the state will "wither away" in the manner familiar in the dogmas of theoretical communism. The state and its historical functions will certainly survive. Just as the traditional security functions of the state survived (and expanded vastly) with the development of the welfare state, so the established welfare functions of the state will survive (and conceivably expand) in the era of the postwelfare state. The key point is that the social environment of the future will see the evolution of new forms of social action, which are largely outside the structure of the state and call for new structures, to handle the "problems of the day." The mechanisms for dealing effectively with the items on the public agenda of the postwelfare state (its schedule of burning issues) call for a combination of (1) a revision and decentralized redeployment of state activities together with (2) the evolution of new, increasingly influential and important, nonstate approaches.

To speak of the "characteristic mission" of the postwelfare order, its generally accepted objectives for realization by the social arrangements of the day, is thus not to maintain that the key role here lies with "the state," with central government rather than local government or even duly encouraged and canalized private initiative. To speak of *aims* alone is to leave the issue of *means* undecided and to prepare the way for a "pragmatic" approach that views the problem of the best way to achieve objectives not as a theoretical or ideological question but one that is strictly practical and empirical. And indeed, the very structure of the needs of the postwelfare period militate toward nongovernmental approaches. The needs of its context in large measure relate to *procedural* issues: a mutuality of common concern in place of a shift of responsibility to the impersonal agencies of government, the enlistment of the humane enthusiasms of people to counteract depersonalization, the facilitation of opportunities for groups and individuals, and the creation of affirmative motivations to make use of these opportunities. Correspondingly, only a penchant for symmetry prevents speaking of a postwelfare *society* rather than *state* to indicate that the new era has as a characteristic a certain deemphasis of the role of government, a demotion from its strikingly prominent status in the earlier, welfare-oriented period. Insofar as the new cluster of preeminent sociopolitical problems lies beyond the centralized grasp of the state, it correspondingly calls for other instrumentalities of solution. The contribution of the state to the handling of these problems will largely be *indirect*, in that the state, rather than playing the lead role of itself arranging solutions, now plays a merely supporting role of facilitating the arrangement of solutions by other social institutions. In its postwelfare role, the state may thus decline in status from a leading "heavy" to a relatively more minor—though doubtless still omnipresent—player on the societal stage.

In the postwelfare era the characteristic problems of the welfare state will certainly not be solved. Social problems are never "solved." They are like the problems of the individual: some are outgrown (e.g., the anxieties of the teen-ager), others are outlived (e.g., the cares of parenthood), and yet others one simply comes to terms with and "learns to live with" until in the fullness of time they resolve themselves in one way or another. But they are always succeeded by other and different problems, problems not actually "new" at all, but the same in essentials from generation to generation. In the era of the postwelfare state, the problems of the welfare state will surely still be with us, even as the security problems of the traditional state survive in the era of the welfare state. The old problems are there, still, as ever, unsolved; it is just that new ones are at the center of emphasis. In the postwelfare era, the old issues of physical and economic security will still be present in the background, but the center of the stage will be held by yet another task—that of forging the conditions for a full and rewarding life in the mass environment of a technologically advanced society.

In an interesting recent paper, "The Need for a New Political Theory,"[11] Lawrence K. Frank develops the theme that the "welfare state" with its bottom-of-the-ladder-oriented aura of charity and philanthropy will give rise to a "service state" that seeks to en-

11. *Daedalus*, Summer 1967.

hance the well-being of everyone. While there is much in this analysis of the need for a new political theory that appears from our standpoint as right and congenial, there is one aspect to which Frank's analysis in terms of general systems theory—viewing the state as a single cohesive system of mutually adjusted parts—does not do sufficient justice. For it would seem that *neither* the traditional model of the state in terms of a mechanical equilibrium *nor* the new organistic model seen in terms of a systems standpoint is an adequate basis for a new form of political order. Frank writes:

As a result of these recent approaches, there is a growing realization that the familiar statement "the whole is greater than the sum of its parts" is misleading and invalid when applied to social organizations. This axiom assumes that the "parts" are more or less homogeneous units that can be aggregated and added as a quantitative ensemble. But the so-called "parts" of a system or organization are its highly differentiated components and participants, each of which has specialized but coupled activities whereby the whole is generated and maintained.[12]

Thus even with the proposed "new look," the old (Hegelian) picture of the social order as *one unified whole*—the coherent expression of a unifying purpose—is still with us. But this thesis is highly questionable. As we see it, the new social order will not take the form of a single monolithic unit at all—neither a machine with meshing parts nor an organism with mutually attuned subsystems. Rather, it will be a polycentric, highly diversified plurality of discrete units, which are independent and disjointed, without many traces of that mutual accordance and adjustment that make for the mutually coordinated social unification near and dear to the heart of organismic political theorists of the Hegelian stamp. *Diversification* is the order of the day in the sociopolitical system of the postindustrial society. Its political and social problems call for solution through highly localized and variegated instrumentalities —instrumentalities with respect to which the centralized state is largely ineffectual.[13] The orderly fusion of diverse elements often

12. Ibid., p. 815.
13. Nor will this decentralization and diversification be confined to the politico-socioeconomic area to the exclusion of that of culture. Regional and communal

called "social orchestration" is one of the key problems of the post-welfare era. The welfare state concerned itself primarily with *uniformities*, with equality, equity, and the like. The key theories of the postwelfare era revolve about diversification, and we will see a new emphasis on the subcultures, regionalisms, and parochialisms of a pluralistic society. The forging of social cohesion amid the multiplicity and variety needed for a full life in a mass society is beyond doubt a central problem of the postwelfare state.

The social ethos of the postwelfare state will thus differ in fundamental ways from that of its predecessor. The welfare state has been characterized primarily by two features: its preoccupation with economic issues of production (full employment) and distribution (economic justice), and its stress on uniformity and egalitarianism. Correspondingly, its social outlook has thus been emphatically democratic. However, the social outlook of the postwelfare state will differ from this pattern in important respects. The new focus of concern will be with the quality of life in both the artistic, self-improvement-oriented and the hedonic, enjoyment-oriented sectors. There will, accordingly, be some turning away from uniformitarianism toward a new stress on diversity of self-development. In these regards there will be a return to an older, rather more aristocratic than democratic point of view. This return to an aristocratic value outlook of course relates only to a narrow sector thereof, that concerned with self-realization, personal improvement, enjoyment, and diversity; the acceptance of socioeconomic inequalities is definitely not at issue. It is a matter of creating for all—or at least for many—certain environmental conditions once limitedly available to only the fortunate few. In its more emphatic stress on the creation of incentives for self-development, and especially for self-improvement in the pursuit of excellence, the postwelfare state reemphasizes a key aspect of an aristocratic perspective.

It is to be hoped—"predicted" is far too strong a word here—that the society of the postwelfare era will also take on one further aspect of the aristocratic concept of obligation (*noblesse oblige*)

---

diversity and the parochialisms of the American melting pot will surely reappear at the forefront of public interest and concern.

in assuming to a greater degree than heretofore patronage of the arts, science, learning, and the works of culture and civilization in general. In particular, an enlivened social concern for the quality of life could well reflect itself in support of the traditional cultural activities: concerts, opera, museums, and the classical stage. The situation in the United States in this regard—even in the current era of an affluent welfare state—is far from encouraging. Every European country has its state opera house and state theater, sometimes administered by the state directly, sometimes by an independent arts council, but invariably supported by public funds. In the United States, the matter rests in a comparatively sad condition: our concert orchestras, opera houses, and museums are slowly starving to death amid general affluence. The Congress balks at a year's allotment of $40 million for the support of the arts and humanities in a nation that spends $300 million on chewing gum. A recent study of the symphony orchestras of major American cities reveals their desperate financial straits: twenty-five of them are expected to close during the 1970s.[14] Even though faced with the pressing social problems of the day—problems that are ever present in some shape or form—no self-respecting nation can shirk its duty of assuring that the heritage of its culture and civilization survives into the hopefully better years that lie ahead. At any rate, the postwelfare era will exhibit a climate of thought vastly more receptive toward this objective than that of the welfare state, since in that era society will come to see its leading challenge in terms of enhancement in the quality of life rather than the cure of social maladies. From this standpoint, it indeed appears that the extent of public acceptance of governmental support of the cultural sector affords something of a test case of the transition from the welfare to the postwelfare era.

The view of the preceding paragraph will doubtless meet with the protest: "If the public really wants museums and concerts and

14. Delos Smith, "Symphony Peril," *Pittsburgh Press*, Feb. 1, 1970. The report's survey of possible ways of forestalling these results goes on to say ("realistically" enough) that government support is not to be looked for in view of "the overwhelming social and economic problems" with which government must cope. (The deeper issue of whether such support can only be justified once all problems of this character have been resolved is, of course, left untouched.)

that sort of thing, let them support it through personal participation and contributions. Why should the instrumentalities of society deploy limited public resources to provide people—indeed a relatively small proportion of people—with something they are unwilling to go out and buy for themselves?" It is important to note that we are not inclined to adopt this line of thought with regard to education, public parks, and highways. We have come in various contexts to take the view that the realization of many social desiderata is a matter for the social implementation of a general concern and is not to be left to the vagaries of individual interest as reflected through personal decisions in the marketplace. There is a pretty well-established consensus that the "free market" operates imperfectly with regard to the so-called *public* goods and services of the collective welfare sector—education, public health, transportation, slum clearance, and the like. In this area the instrumentalities of society have generally played a role of substantial significance. A *community* of interests being involved, the aristic dimension of the "quality of life" is also not merely a private desideratum but a properly social concern. Why the cultural sector should be treated as fundamentally different from the recreational, as reflected in publicly maintained parks, wildlife preserves, and the like, is, to say the least, obscure.

A major—perhaps the main—problem (or, rather, problem family) that faces the postwelfare state is that of untying the knot of the modern city, of devising the means to tame and civilize urban life.[15] Even the casual visitor's views of the surface features of a city generally suffices for a diagnosis of its strengths and ills—indeed, is in some ways better than seeing the matter from the inside, since deficiencies are most striking before familiarity has bred the acceptance of resignation. Agreeable surroundings that please the eye and ear (and nose!), the availability of amenities (schools, parks, transportation, sports, and cultural facilities), the cooperation and mutual helpfulness of people—or the lack of these desiderata—can be brought out by little more than the casual inspec-

---

15. For an excellent assessment of the needs of American cities and the means for meeting them, see Edmund K. Faltermayer, *Redoing America* (New York, 1968).

tion of a tourist's ramble. Everyone is by now familiar with the depressing catalogue of the problems of urban America at the present day: dirt, noise, snarled traffic, physical ugliness, crowding, crime, friction in interpersonal contacts. The corresponding results have often been discussed and lamented: personal demoralization, group tensions, and the social alienation that comes about when people interact with others not as people but as parts of a system. These conditions have conspired to produce an anomalous result: "Uniquely in human history, Americans have been evacuating their cities not because there is an invader at the gates but because they are less and less viable as communities in which to work and raise families."[16] A prime task of the postwelfare society is to devise means of securing pleasantness for urban life—to restore convenience to city living, to make the city physically attractive, to decompose it (insofar as possible) into units of human scale, to facilitate civility in interpersonal dealings under the crowded conditions of mass interaction, etc.

Here, then, we have one typical example of the reorientation of the focus of society's attention that will characterize the situation of the postwelfare state. In the era of the welfare state, society's attention was directed to the basics needed to make life *viable* on a mass basis in the context of a developed industrial economy. With the postwelfare state, the prime task will be that of making the circumstances of life *richer and fuller* for a mass population in the context of a "postindustrial" economy oriented heavily toward the production of services rather than goods. The welfare state saw its problem in terms of making life in a mass society physically and economically *secure*; the postwelfare state faces the enormously more difficult and challenging problem of making it socially more *civilized*, personally *fuller*, and environmentally more *pleasant*. Accomplishment of this monumental task will tax to the utmost the resources of leadership that even a clever and resourceful peo-

16. Harry K. Girvetz in *Encyclopedia of the Social Sciences*, s.v. "Welfare State," see p. 519. This phenomenon is the source of the financial dilemma of the modern American city—a vast expenditure for costly municipal and social services in the face of a drastic balance-of-payments problems as more and more well-paid workers become commuters who depend on the city for their jobs but pay most of their taxes in the suburbs.

ple can muster. Only the inspiration of leadership can forge that coordination and cooperation without which social goals—those of the postwelfare era included—can never come to concrete realization. Order and system in human affairs do not emerge magically by themselves from the independent, uncoordinated activities of men pursuing their diverse purposes in separate ways. Be its aim to fulfill the requirements of welfare or to transcend them, a purposeful social order is never a purely spontaneous growth but always a delicate contrivance forged by men working in concert for the realization of an ideal.

NAME INDEX

SUBJECT INDEX

Name Index

Adenauer, Konrad, 91
Anderson, Stanford, 137n

Barry, Brian, 78n, 115n, 129n, 146n
Bauer, Raymond, 73n
Becker, G. S., 7n, 81n, 167n
Bell, Daniel, 137, 138n, 166
Benn, S. I., 10n, 21n, 146n
Bentham, Jeremy, 10
Berdayev, Nicholas, 62n
Bindoff, S. T., 3n
Booth, Charles, 94
Boulding, Kenneth, 56n
Bradburn, N. M., 41n, 79, 89-90
Braithwaite, R. B., 31n
Braybrooke, David, 19n, 122n, 124n, 142, 142n, 146n
Bryden, H. A., 20n
Buchanan, J. M., 69n
Buhler, Charlotte, 69n
Burnham, David, 35n
Butler, Samuel, 44n

Cantril, Hadley, 41n, 45, 70
Caplovitz, David, 79, 89-90
Carnap, Rudolf, 105n
Carson, Rachel, 132
Clements, T. S., 36n
Coleman, W. E., 69n
Costello, T. W., 43n, 47n
Cromwell, Oliver, 21n
Cyert, R. M., 43n

Dalkey, N. C., 40n, 60n
Darley, J. M., 33n
De Gaulle, Charles, 91
Descartes, René, 118n
Drewnowski, Jan, 74
Dublin, L. I., 81n
Dubos, René, 79n, 84n

Eisenhower, Milton S., 52n
Erskine, Hazel, 41n

Faltermayer, Edmund, 177n
Fedorenko, N. P., 30n
Fein, Rashi, 81n
Feld, Sheila, 41n
Fellows, E. W., 70
Frank, L. K., 173-74
Fuchs, V. R., 93n, 102n, 105, 109n

Galbraith, J. K., 15, 121
Gillespie, R. D., 70
Girvetz, H. K., 4n, 151n, 178n
Green, T. F., 117n
Gross, B. M., 60n, 73n, 160n
Gurin, Gerald, 41n

Harrington, Michael, 64, 96n, 97-98, 101n, 106, 109, 111n, 153
Harsanyi, J. C., 31n
Hinrichs, H. A., 82n
Hobsbawn, E. J., 93n
Hobson, J. A., 19, 96n
Hunter, Robert, 95n

Subject Index